C000180473

STEAM IN THE VEINS

FRONT COVER ILLUSTRATION

The Author driving one of his Fowler engines to the Great Missenden rally in the 1970's.

STEAM IN THE VEINS

Being an account of memories of the
Boughton Family Business and related happenings
in the Chiltern Hills.

by

John H Boughton O.B.E., O.St. J.

Published by John Boughton
Kingsweir, 69 Amersham Road,
Little Chalfont, Bucks. HP6 6SP

Hard Back ISBN 0 9516378 1 9
Soft Back ISBN 0 9516378 0 0

In Memory of my beloved father

T.T.B

All rights reserved.
No portion of this book may be reproduced
by any process whatsoever without the permission
in writing of the publisher.

CONTENTS

List of Illustrations

All photos are from the Author's collection except where otherwise stated.

INTRODUCTION

The author relaxes with a "Foden" timber tractor during a week-end break in wartime.
Photo John Mullett.

This is the story of a country business, founded in the Chiltern Hills countryside by a countryman, told by his son who was born and bred in the country and who spent his life in country pursuits and interests.

It is a simple story, into which the theme of steam engines is woven, partly because the business was based on steam power but more importantly because steam engines in general and traction engines in particular played such an important role in the lives of the writer and his father.

The writer wishes to thank all those who have helped and encouraged him to carry out this work, especially his beloved wife Betty, and gratefully acknowledges the help and advice of many friends and wellwishers who took an interest in its production.

Particular thanks are extended to Mrs. Mullett, widow of John, who so kindly gave permission for some of her late husband's photos to be included in the book.

The design of the front cover by Bill Macbeth and his work on the layout, assisted so enthusiastically by Michelle Eastwood are also much appreciated.

CHAPTER I

ENVIRONMENT

River Chess, Latimer.

It is difficult to imagine a more attractive place for a boy to be brought up than in the Chiltern Hills, especially that area around Chenies and Latimer where I was born and where my family had roots going back for so many years.

My father ran his business on the high ground between the Chess and Misbourne valleys, at Amersham Common. The word Common was a misnomer by the time he moved there around the year 1906, as the term applied to the district before the Land Enclosure Act, and there had been no common as such in living memory.

At that time ours was the only house in Bell or Beel Lane as it probably should be called in view of its close proximity to Beel House, a country residence adjoining the main Hatfied to Reading turnpike road.

The hamlet, for it was little more, straggled rather untidily along the main road and there were a few houses in Finch Lane, behind the White Lion public house, where our nearest neighbours the Goodsons lived.

Our home was, to us, an oasis surrounded by large estates. Lord Chesham, from whom my father had bought his property, had his estates to the north of us, and the Duke of Bedford owned the Chenies Estate to the east. In those days, before the developers arrived, we were in deep tranquil country, enjoying simple pleasures and breathing the pure clean fresh air of the open country.

Beech woods in the Chilterns.

The whole district was, and still is, criss-crossed by a maze of footpaths and bridle ways, threading through some of the most beautiful countryside imaginable including the Chess Valley and the beech woods bordering it. The valley must always have been attractive because the Romans chose to settle there, and the beauty has been enhanced by the formation of lakes, waterfalls and gardens of the Latimer estate.

Every season is unique, and my brother and I, together with our friends made the most of our opportunities to explore and enjoy the countryside, rambling with our wire-haired fox terrier "Pip", over the length and breadth of the hills and valleys which formed our habitat.

Winter had, and always will have, a beauty all of its own, especially when the hoar-frost was on the trees and the lakes and ponds were frozen over, and we ran to keep warm.

Looking back I think that spring time was the best, when the Bucks beech trees burst into life, the woods were carpeted with bluebells and the foliage took on the fresh light green hues which always remind me of Easter and resurrection.

And what woods they were in those days before World War Two came to decimate them. Beech trees seventy or more feet tall, over a metre in diameter, standing like columns in a cathedral chancel, stretching at least three miles from Raans Farm to Chenies all along the ridge above Latimer and on the surrounding high ground. The text books on forestry high lighted them as the prime example of the best beech trees in England, and I have no doubt that they were correct.

John Henry Boughton (the author's Grandfather) of Chenies Manor on horse-back in "The Lady Cheney Walks, Chenies".

The shade from these enormous sentinels kept the woodlands cool, even during the hottest days of summer. It was a joy to wander through the glades down to the water meadows where we could paddle in the streams, and keeping a sharp lookout for water bailiffs and keepers, try our hand at tickling for the trout which abounded in the river.

As the seasons progressed the woods became objects of exquisite beauty, the autumn tints and colours surpassing human imagination, before the chill winds came and the whole majestic canopy came tumbling to the forest floor, to form a carpet the best part of a foot deep. Travelling through the wooded trails took on a new dimension when the leaves had fallen and it was rather like wading in the sea; shuffling, rather than walking or running, whilst "Pip", with his shortish legs had to resort to bounding and jumping, barking excitedly as he went.

Family group including "Pip" at the feet of the author.

We were not confined to the beaten track, as my father's brother, our uncle Harry, was tenant of three farms on the Chenies Estate and my mother's brothers George and William were responsible for two others. Furthermore, my father's business involved the threshing of corn on farms for miles around, so, one way and another, we had access to a very wide territory and we came to know it well.

As though the countryside were not sufficient in itself to occupy our time and attention, we had the added bonus of the Great Central Railway which passed our home. From our garden we could watch the trains go by and wave to the drivers and firemen who never failed to return our greetings.

We were a closely knit happy family, surviving as best we could through the long years of depression following World War One, which created so many problems for employers and employees alike.

And then there were my father's engines for ever coming and going as he catered for the varying needs of the agricultural and commercial community; steam engines of all sorts and sizes, each with its own characteristics, designed or adapted to carry out the requirements of the district in a way befitting the industrial revolution. Altogether there was a wealth of interest and experience just waiting to be absorbed and we took to it naturally, much as a duck takes to water.

CHAPTER II

FAMILY AND BUSINESS ROOTS

Dodd's Mill, Chenies.

Members of the Boughton family have been involved with the running of water mills, farms and businesses in or near the Chess valley for nearly two hundred years. However, it was romance and not business that brought them there in the first place. Mary Boughton married George Dodd of Chenies Mill on 20th March 1797, and her sister Sarah Boughton married Richard Elliot of Bois Mill, at Chenies Church, on 31st March 1800. Their niece, another Sarah Boughton, married John, son of George and Mary Dodd and lived a long and fulfilled life at Chenies at what is now known as Dodd's Mill, where my brother lives. The latter part of her life was spent as a widow and she had no issue.

Eventually the running of the mill and the adjoining farm became a burden to her and she appealed for help to her brother Thomas Boughton of Ashendon, near Aylesbury, who had several sons, the eldest of whom John, was about to leave the Lord William School at Thame. It was agreed that he should help his Aunt and he accordingly moved to Chenies. On 25th October 1871 he married Kate Harper, a farmer's daughter from Wotton Underwood, near Ashendon, and moved into the "Manor Farm" at Chenies, where my family farmed until 1932. He also took over the tenancy of the Mill and the "Mill Farm" when Sarah died in 1881 as well as the "Old House Farm", all of which were owned by the Duke of Bedford and formed part of the Chenies Estate. He had five children. My father Thomas Trafford Boughton, was his eldest son and throughout his life he was affectionally known as T.T.B.

Tom was fascinated by steam engines from a very early age. The nursery in the old Manor House where he was born was papered on all four walls with cuttings from papers and journals of the day, and whilst it is true that some illustrated bloodcurdling scenes of military actions, most of them as I remember, treated on the theme of traction engines and their environment.

As a boy, he sought to assuage his appetite for knowledge on the subject, by sending away to maufacturers of engines for catalogues of their products. It was a matter of some embarrassment on one occasion, when a representative of a well known maker arrived at the farm in a horse and trap. He had travelled from Basingstoke to follow up the enquiry, only to be introduced to a red faced boy by his father who knew nothing of what his son had been up to.

Tom Boughton as a young man.

The majority of the work on the farms was carried out by horses but contractors were employed to thresh the crops and steam-plough the land to supplement the horses. It became apparent that, as he grew up, Tom was more interested in the engines and the machinery at the Mill than in other aspects of farming. He made it his business to get to know the drivers of road locomotives that passed along the main Hatfield to Reading turnpike road, hard by the farm, and gained some hands-on experience from them. There was not much that he did not know about traction engines by the time he came of age.

Fanny Boughton the author's beloved mother.

Tom founded our business in 1897 having persuaded his father to buy him a threshing set with its round from the widow of one Clark of Chalfont, who was the contractor that carried out the threshing on the Chenies farms. For nine years he operated from his father's farm at the Manor but by the year 1906 he was sufficiently established to acquire land at Bell Lane from Lord Chesham and moved his business there. His father continued to farm at Chenies until he died in 1915. My father's brother Harry carried on the farms until he retired in 1932.

In 1912 Tom married the lovely Fanny Smith from Lodge Farm on the Chenies estate, built his house at his place of business and settled down to raise a family. They had two sons, Trafford and John, as well as a daughter Joan.

Looking back and remembering the topics of conversation when Uncle Harry Boughton and his wife, Auntie Flo visited us for tea every Thursday afternoon, I realise that, in many ways, things have not changed in the domestic scene over the last sixty-five years or so. The cherries still sink to the bottom of home made cakes and the difficult decisions arising out of the choice of recipes for various options of marmalade still have to be taken. Intricate knitting patterns still have to be deciphered and instructions to the gardener as to exactly when to prune the rose trees have to be timed precisely. Questions concerning the education of children and the choice of schools will not go away and the venue for the summer holidays has to be decided upon. These things have not changed and probably never will.

Chapter III

EARLY MEMORIES

Boughton Patent Folding Hay Sweep invented by my father about 1900 with his home the Manor House, Chenies in background.

There has never been a time in my life in which steam engines did not feature in one way or another. Our family home was at my father's place of business and we only had to go through the gate at the bottom of our garden to enter into an Aladdin's cave of interest and fascination in the form of engines, some in steam and some under repair.

Family and business life were inseparably mixed up together. The head of the family was the head of the business, and the fortunes and misfortunes of the latter were followed closely by all of us. When the office closed, the telephone (number Amersham Common 5) was switched through to the house, and demanded instant attention regardless of all other considerations. There was no escaping its insistent summons by day or night.

Bell Lane was a long way from the nearest services and apart from the telephone, which was a mixed blessing, we were devoid of mains electricity, gas, water and drainage. All these facilities, apart from gas, which we never had, were provided "in house".

Electric light came to us by kind permission of a temperamental stationary engine, which ran on parafin. The combustion of fuel was aided by a hot bulb which had to be heated by an enormous blow lamp during the starting-up operation, which was a messy and time consuming affair, requiring a great deal of patience, energy and "know how".

Grandpa John Boughton with his Grandson Trafford posed in transport of the day.

The electricity was stored in large open-topped batteries with glass casings. In order to check whether they were up to strength, a floating Hydrometer was placed from cell to cell, and it was always a thrill to go in to the battery house to see this operation carried out, as the acid gave off a gas that made your eyes run and your nose and throat tingle. Rain was our sole source of water and as steam engines were thirsty contraptions every drop was precious. Large underground storage reservoirs provided a buffer stock but sometimes during a long hot summer they were exhausted and supplies had to brought in from the river. All our drinking water had to be filtered and/or boiled.

On the subject of toilet facilities in the works I will not dwell, except to say that they were primitive, and that most employees preferred to smoke strong pipe tobacco when visiting them. I am glad to record that the facilities in our home were more up to date.

Local transport was catered for by horse and trap, a means that my mother used to visit her sisters in Chesham but we also had a car for more distant excursions. The earliest one that I can remember was a Fiat, but before that my father had a De Dion Bouton and an Arghyll. Later we changed to Humbers of which we had a whole series, culminating in a "Snipe" which was a super machine.

A typical spread of steam rollers with "Copper Knob" the roller on the left of picture. Owner T.T.B.

The Fiat was an open tourer; had a long bonnet, and Acetylene head lamps, beautifully made of brass. The windscreen was vertical and the seats were high. It was a far cry from the sleek, stream-lined creations of modern times, but it ran well and up to the time I started school, I travelled a great deal in it with my father as he visited his business interests over a wide area.

By that time he had been established for nearly twenty years and was operating some twenty or so steam engines of one kind or another. Many of these engines were steam rollers for which there was a good demand in those years immediately after the first World War. The roads all over the country were being upgraded to accept the increasing population of motor cars which were rapidly replacing horse drawn traffic.

Seated comfortably on my father's knee, wrapped in a warm travelling rug, driven by the tall young Frank Honour, who had gained his experience handling ambulances on the Western Front a few years earlier, we would set off on the long journey to the Dover road in Kent where a number of the rollers were working.

The first few miles were through country roads, well clipped hedges, and the sleepy villages of Chalfont St. Giles and Chalfont St. Peter, then down the Misbourne valley to the main London to Oxford Road after which we were soon into Uxbridge where the tram tracks started.

A Ruston Steam Digger similar but smaller than those used on the Dover Road. Photo depicts digger restored and owned by Mr. Ian Woollett.

From then on the density of traffic began to build up as we approached the great Metropolis and by the time we crossed the Thames at Vauxhall bridge driving became really hectic. Slow moving horse drawn wagons and drays abounded and there were hundreds of open-topped double decker buses with solid tyred wheels competing with the trams for space on the overcrowded roads and streets as they transported the teeming masses of Londoners from one part of the conurbation to another. Our intrepid driver coped well with the complications as we threaded our way, in dense traffic, through the bright lights of New Cross and Lewisham.

The big attractions were the electric illuminations and advertisments, flashing their messages in countless sequences and patterns, simulating everything from flowing liquids to chorus girls, as they promoted the sales of various goods, services and attractions that the great city had to offer.

At last we reached the open Dover Road where still more interests awaited us. Our steam rollers were consolidating the batter on Farningham and Wrotham Hills where massive road works were in progress. Enormous "Ruston" Steam Navvies were tearing the heart out of deep cuttings towards the top of the hills and the soil was taken by contractors' steam locomotives to areas where embankments were being built lower down.

Tasker Roller driven by Bert Gaylor who travelled with his wife and family, all living together in the living van. Owner T.T.B. Photo author's collection.

When the steam diggers were hard at work they were a joy to watch. Smoke from their funnels was supplemented by rushes of steam as their safety valves lifted and mists of condensate surrounded the operation as the main, slewing and monkey engines sporadically burst into life and exhausted steam to the atmosphere. The whole scene gave the impression of great urgency as whilst the diggers fussily went about their business, the steam locos manoeuvred the wagons into position for the giant monsters to disgorge mouthful after mouthful of chalk into them with a minumum of interruption or delay.

Meanwhile teams of men were dispersing and spreading the soil on the land being built up and our steam rollers pounded it down to form the base for the new road. The drivers of the rollers lived in vans which they towed behind their charges. Some travelled with their wives and families. Others spent the week on the site and went home at week-ends often cycling twenty or thirty miles each way, according to where they were working.

Hot water was provided from the boiler feed injectors on the engines, and to this day I never smell carbolic soap without thinking of those characters, who so long ago, after a hard day on their engines, stripped to the waist and washed from buckets by the side of the Dover Road.

A group of Boughton employees. Note the clay pipes.

Many of the drivers wore mole skin trousers with flop fronts which were a kind of uniform for the real "died in the wool" steam engine fraternity.

Clay pipes were also popular with these men who kept them gripped firmly between their teeth most of the time but seldom lit them, and more often than not they were upside down anyway.

The scenes on the Dover Road were repeated all over England as the gradients on roads through hilly country were tamed and made safer. Brentford, Denham, Dashwood Hill near High Wycombe, and Benson Oxon, to name but a few, were all places that witnessed these exciting if transient activities, which remain printed so indelibly on my memory.

After attending to the business of the day we headed for home in the old Fiat, battling our way through the rush hour London traffic after dark, calling at a Lyons tea shop in New Cross for sustenance on the way.

Of the return journeys I can recall little else as, after an exciting and exhausting day, I was tired out and fell to sleep curled up on my father's lap for most of the journey back.

Chapter IV

GROWING UP

The author as a Grammar School boy in centre of picture with Teddy Birch on his left and Bert Oxborrow with his nephew and niece on his right. The owner of the Burrell is on extreme right of picture which was taken near Ipswich circa 1929.

After the freedom and variety that I had enjoyed as a very young boy, school came as an anti-climax. My parents had done their best to prepare me for the experience and had given me the impression that going to school was something to look forward to. I remember coming home at the end of the first day with the firm idea that, for me, learning would have to be endured rather than enjoyed. The thought of spending the next decade at school appalled me and I made the stupid mistake of wishing my time away.

My brother had already started his education and I joined him at Kingsley School, which was run by two godly sisters the Misses Lilian and Constance Brown. We received a good grounding in the three "R"s and learnt to recite passages from the Bible. It still comes naturally for me to say, "All we like sheep have gone astray: we have turned every one to his own way; and the Lord has laid on Him the iniquity of us all".

I had been given a new bicycle, so we cycled the two miles to school, my big brother shepherding me and teaching me to observe the rules of the road. There was very little traffic in those days and we never came to any harm.

When I was ten I graduated to Dr. Challoner's Grammar School, along with some of my friends from our prep school, and at the age of sixteen, after a spell at the Tutorial College in Red Lion Square, London, I left school altogether. It had not been so bad after all.

15

"Moonlight" Aveling Compound, 4755 one of the eight engines used at Addiscombe during the tree clearing operation. Photo illustrates the engine delivering logs to Fitzgerald's sawmill in Bellingdon Road, Chesham Circa 1920. Driver Dickie Groom, owner T.T.B.

The great thing about school was the holidays as I could always be sure that there were plenty of interesting things to do. I had made some good friends both in and out of school and the countryside offered many distractions to us in the form of bird's nesting, (at which my friend Ray Brothers was particularly adept), fishing, cycling and following the fox hounds. All these activities were punctuated and supplemented by excursions connected with the business in which steam engines were an essential ingredient, and whenever we liked we could talk our way into a trip.

During the mid-twenties the whole country was in the midst of an economic depression and much innovation was needed to keep the business viable and the cash flow positive. Work of all sorts was taken on and anything to keep the men and machines earning was considered and sought after.

One unusual opportunity presented itself in the Croydon area. Addiscombe Park was to be made into a super golf course. Hundreds of mature trees were obstructing the line of the fairways and needed uprooting and removing. It was a big job but my father took it on. The work occupied one Spring and Summer, involving eight traction engines, a sawmill on the site, and about thirty men who lived in caravans in the park.

Trips to Addiscombe were the highlights of our holidays that year. It was a glorious setting and as we made our way down the beautiful drive we were rewarded by the sight of the mansion in its splendid surroundings with the largest spreading Cedar tree in England gracing the front lawn.

Mann steam tractor used for ploughing by direct traction, sawing and forestry but mostly for consolidating in-fill on major road building contracts. Driver John Brightman, Owner T.T.B.

The journey to Croydon took about one and a half hours and we usually travelled with the manager of the project. On arrival, as long as we maintained a low profile and kept our heads down well back from the action, we were free to explore the Park and amuse ourselves to our hearts' content.

In those days the tree was not the sacred symbol that it it today. There was no such thing as a tree preservation order, no town and country planners, no environmental protection groups, and no laws to prevent the owners of trees cutting them down when they so desired. The day of the golf addict had dawned and everything that stood in the line of the little white ball had to go, however old, splendid and beautiful. We saw trees uprooted in minutes that had taken two hundred years to grow. We witnessed them being dismembered by axemen as soon as they fell and we saw them being hauled to the steam driven mill by our traction engines to be sawn and quartered. The roots were piled into heaps and burned.

There was much to see and do and the time passed quickly. All we had to worry about was reporting back to the car at an appointed time for the journey home.

The scenes and activities were constantly changing, the wages had to be paid and work had to be found for men and machines. Large acreages of arable land had been laid or fallen down to grass, reducing the demand for ploughing and threshing. Many of the steamrollers had returned to base as road work was curtailed because of the economic slump. Times were hard and many men were out of work, a situation that some found it hard to accept, especially those who had endured the hardships, privations and horrors of World War 1.

"Moonlight" driving a 10" Gwynn Centrifugal pump at Laleham. The name of this engine arose because it had the reputation of being involved in work by night as well as day.

It was therefore, with a sense of relief that work opened up for the engines in connection with the installation of the electrical grid in the Thames Valley. Pirelli, the civil engineers and electrical contractors had secured the contract for the erection of pylons through the valley. It was winter and the water table was high. The line crossed some of the wettest country in the area of Staines and Lalehem, and attempts to excavate the foundations of the pylons were doomed almost before they began as water flooded in.

The problem caused headaches for the contractors but presented a fine opportunity for my father who lost no time in exploiting the situation by offering his services to provide large steam driven centrifugal pumps to keep the water level down long enough for the concrete foundations to be poured.

Traction engines are very adaptable workhorses and can be used for many chores, such as hauling loads, winching over trees and utilising their flywheels and governors to drive any belt operated machinery such as threshers, chaff-cutters and pumps, to name but a few.

Hempstead Portable Pumping.

This engine was originally supplied when new to Egypt and was returned to England after completing an assignment. It was purchased second hand by T.T.B. who used it for many years for pumping and driving a portable sawmill. The boy in the picture is Master Trafford Boughton as he was known at that time.

Pumping provided a useful amount of revenue and often created work for machinery and men during gaps in activities. Foundations for bridges and buildings of all sorts often needed to be pumped out whilst they were being constructed especially in low lying waterlogged areas near rivers.

Stationary pumps were also installed at Locks on the Grand Union Canal and during times of drought T.T.B. hired out his engines to the Canal Company to drive them.

The versatility of the steam traction engines enabled many of the same road locomotives that had carried out the Addiscombe Park saga, to drive the pumps at Laleham. The scenario was entirely different however, as the battle against ingress of water to the sumps had to be fought continuously, day and night, weekday and Sunday, once the work on each individual pylon had started until it was completed. The drivers worked in shifts, and the fires in the boilers were not damped down for weeks on end.

Fortunately, from some points of view, it was a bitterly cold winter and the ground was frozen solid for much of the time. Whilst such conditions were tough to endure and caused great hardships for all those engaged on the contract, they nevertheless solved the problem of traversing the swamps with heavy equipment which would have created tremendous difficulties otherwise.

19

Boughton Winch stringing overhead wires onto pylons.

It was in such Arctic conditions that I visited the way-leave with my father after dark on a clear starlit night. The cold was intense but the operation was in full swing. Acetylene flares were everywhere, lighting not only the operations at each pylon, but the tracks in between, over which contractor's six wheeled Thorneycroft trucks churned their way as they fed stores and supplies to the men toiling in the sumps, digging away at the foundations under appalling conditions.

I sometimes wonder when I switch on the lights at home whether any of us appreciate the toil, effort and sacrifice that has gone into the provision of a boon which we take so very much for granted.

As a boy I could not possibly envisage the important part that the electrical industry would play in connection with our business in later life. It did not occur to me to enquire how the wires would be strung through the pylons or how they would be tensioned and maintained.

In the event I found myself responsible for developing winches especially built for the industry and had the satisfaction of selling them and seeing them operate successfully in many countries of the world. The winches are fitted to trucks and tractors and are made in versions designed to string electric wires above and below ground.

The "Boughton" RB44 four wheel drive truck is also widely used in the industry and the electricity boards are among our most valued customers.

Chapter V

THE GREAT CENTRAL RAILWAY (L.N.E.R. from 1923 onwards)

Double Headed Express storming through the Chilterns. Photo author's collection.

Although I did not realise it at the time, the Great Central Railway was only twenty five years old when I first remember it. The track which it shared with the Metropolitan Railway ran through a cutting hard by my father's works. There were three lines; two carrying the trains to and from Aylesbury and beyond, and one on which the Chalfont Road to Chesham shuttle plied its continuous trade. All the trains were hauled by steam locomotives painted in the liveries of the times. The Metropolitan engines were maroon, the Great Central tank locos hauling the local trains were black, and the express locos which interested me most were apple green. I can see them in my mind's eye to this day, pounding and storming their way hauling heavy trains up the long incline to the summit near Great Missenden before descending through the Wendover Gap in the Chiltern Hills to the Vale of Aylesbury on their long journey to the big cities of the North.

The main line engines all had names and it was a matter of speculation as to which engines would be hauling which expresses on any particular day. Would it be "Sir Sam Fay", "Butler Henderson", "Earl Haig", "Earl Beatty", or was there a chance that it would give us a real thrill and be a double header hauled by two locos in tandem, perhaps "Zeebrugge", "Jutland", "Ypres", "Passchendaele" or "The Somme".

CHALFONT ROAD STATION.

Chalfont Road Station 1922 (Now Chalfont and Latimer). Photo author's collection.

Long before the expresses reached us the beat of the exhausts from the locos could be heard as it was a long pull up the incline from Rickmansworth. The work was hard both on the engines and firemen who were piling the coal into the fireboxes, creating incandescent heat to keep the boiler pressures up to maximum for the duration of the climb.

Sparks and cinders from the chimneys of the locomotives often set fire to dry grass and gorse bushes bordering the track, during the dry summer months. When this happened my brother and I would attack the flames with bass brooms and beat out the blaze before it could jump the fire breaks and spread to our property. The fires were most frequent when the drivers of the Chesham Shuttle attempted to race their counterparts on the main line for the sheer fun of it, no doubt breaking all the rules in the book as they did so.

The trains kept good time and in our works blacksmith's shop which backed on to the railway, the smiths would pause from their hot work as they heard the "Ten to Four" thundering towards them, take out their fob watches, remark on the punctuality of the express, and take the opportunity of drinking tea from their flasks.

Passengers on the train were also taking their tea but in the rather more gracious surroundings of the Restaurant Cars and as a boy I wondered, as I watched them glide past, if I would ever travel in such luxury when I grew up. Little did I know that I was destined to travel on the Royal Scot, The Flying Scotsman, The Cornish Riviera, The Orient Express, The Canadian Pacific Scenic Dome train through the Rockies, the Simplon Express and many other world famous trains in the years ahead.

22

Typical scene on the Great Central Railway in the 1920's. Photo author's collection.

The expresses started from Marylebone Station and in the evenings there was one train, first stop Amersham, which was popular with commuters, if for no other reason than that they could take tea and cucumber sandwiches as they relaxed on the way home.

There were goods trains too, and these caused amusement for us as there were sidings at Chalfont Road Station which formed a miniature marshalling yard where shunting took place and where, on Sunday afternoons we would watch the waggons being manoeuvered into the right sequence for decanting, one or more at a time, further up the line.

The railway was always a focus of interest especially when unusual occurrences created diversions. During the General Strike of 1926 some of the trains were manned by volunteer crews, not all of whom were up to the job. One express ran into trouble at Amersham Station when the amateur driver failed to get the injector to work and ran the boiler short of water. In order to save serious damage to the firebox, the fire was thrown out on to the track, with the result that the sleepers caught fire.

This incident created quite a pantomime and went to show that enthusiasm on its own was not enough to tame the mighty giants into docile work horses.

"Sir Sam Fay" Express Locomotive Great Central Railway. Photo author's collection.

In foggy weather the signalling was supplemented by detonators on the track and we were subjected to intermittent cacophonous explosions as the vital messages were transmitted to the anxious drivers taking their charges through the dense murk and gloom ahead.

When the snow was falling heavily in winter the Chesham Shuttle would run all night to keep the track clear, but in spite of this precaution, on more than one occasion it became stuck in snow drifts in the area of Raans Farm near our home, and had to be dug out by hand. Another time a locomotive broke a connecting rod outside our Works and our wags put up a notice facing the track "Vulcan Engine Works. Locos repaired".

The thrill of watching the expresses coasting down the incline never lost its appeal, and we used to take up a vantage point on the bridge by the Works to see them come into view, the locomotives weaving and swaying gently as they hurtled down the slope at seventy miles an hour or more.

Drivers of the expresses usually gave a long blast on their whistles as they approached our Works, presumably to warn the station staff ahead that they were coming through at high speed and to give passengers, waiting on the platform, time to stand well back.

"Black Jack" hauling manure from Chalfont Road Station to the Chenies Farms in the early 1900s. Photo author's collection.

It was fascinating to listen to the Doppler effect of the whistles as they changed from a shrill note when the trains were approaching, to a lower pitch as they passed under us and receded into the distance. Although we did not know it at the time it was an early introduction to an important scientific principle.

Our relationship with the station staff was good as our business used the railway services both to send and receive goods. A truck load of steam coal arrived in the sidings every week to feed the insatiable appetite of my father's steam engines and he also used the railway to despatch his horse-drawn patent foldable hay sweeps, a product of the Works, to destinations all over the country. As a result of the "entente cordiale" that existed between my father and the railwaymen we were sometimes allowed to visit the signalbox and watch the signalman Mr. Saint heave the levers to change the points and signals.

It was a great sadness when, in the course of his duties whilst crossing the track to give the tablet to the driver of the Chesham Shuttle, he stepped into the path of an express and was killed instantly. At a stroke we had lost a friend. He had also been our bee-keeper, as he tended our hives in his spare time, and he was sadly missed.

The passage of time has completely changed the scene on the railway. The lines are still there but the magic has gone. "Butler Henderson" has survived into preservation but much of the track to the North has been torn up. The dignified long distance travellers have given way to commuters and there are no longer any cucumber sandwiches. It is not the same.

Chapter VI

FAIRGROUNDS

Pettigrove's fine Foster Showman's Engine, a frequent visitor to Amersham Fair.

As far back as I can remember, the fair came to Amersham during the third week in September each year. When I was a boy the stalls and rides occupied the whole length and most of the breadth of the wide high street leaving just enough room for the traffic to squeeze through the town, threading its way between the throngs of enthralled bystanders.

Visitors from far and wide came to enjoy the atmosphere of the country fair, as before the days of television and the universal use of radio, the simple pleasures of the countryside as typified by the fair, took on a greater significance than they do today, or so it seems to me. I remember as a boy overhearing a group of American visitors to the fair; it is not difficult to overhear our brethren from across the Atlantic, and they were saying that they timed their visit to the U.K. each year to coincide with the Amersham Fair, and I can well understand how they felt.

In the early days the Galloping Horses or Roundabouts were powered by their own highly polished steam centre engines complete with a small vertical engine to drive the organ which blared out its intoxicating medley of old time music, punctuated by the whistles from the centre engine, as the contraption gathered speed and the excited riders hung on for dear life.

A Typical Steam Driven Roundabout similar to those used at Amersham.

Most of the roundabouts were built in Norfolk, either by Savages of Kings Lynn or Tidmans, both of which were masters of the art of building fair ground paraphernalia. Like many other makers of steam equipment they emulated Leonado Da Vinci and were not only great engineers but wonderful artists as well.

The beautifully balanced double high pressure centre engines combined with the fine carvings and paintings to produce a ride that was a pleasure to operate and a joy to watch. It is no wonder that some superb examples of these masterpieces have survived into preservation, or that they are still thrilling an admiring public.

There were other rides and preoccupations too, such as coconut shies, pin alleys, hoop-la stalls, swing boats, fortune tellers, rifle ranges, dodgem cars, boxing booths, and competitive games involving the throwing of darts and rolling of coins on to marked out tables very much as they are today, but if anything they were less sophisticated than they are now.

The vendors of the various diversions competed with each other, calling out to attract attention to their particular novelties or merchandise and away in the distance the roar of motor cycle engines could be heard as the trick riders performed unbelievable feats of hair raising skills on the "Wall of Death".

It was a great occasion, and brought a splash of colour and excitement to the town at a time of year when the days were shortening, the autumn leaves were changing to the beautiful hues which herald the onset of winter and the populace were beginning to count the number of shopping days to Christmas.

An example of a Scenic Burrell Showman's at its best.

The whole scene was bathed in bright lights but there was one big difference from the fairs of today; the electric power for the lights and music was generated by large ornate steam road locomotives knows as showman's engines. The cab stays, steering rods and other parts were covered with polished twisted brass, and the cylinders on engines with overhead valves such as Fowlers and Fosters, were lagged with brass sheeting. Brass stars occupied any flat surfaces, such as side motion cover plates, cylinder covers, and belly tanks. There were usually four or more of these beautiful, well cared for polished monsters at the Amersham Fair. When darkness fell they created an unforgettable sight, sound and smell, which cannot be completely re-created on the rally fields of today.

Sometimes when I was small my beloved father would take me to the fair on Saturday night and if I was lucky, I would return with a goldfish, much to my delight but also to the consternation of my dear mother, who knew only too well who would have to look after the fish once the initial thrill of owning it wore off.

However, it was the steam engines rather than the goldfish and coconut shies which were the great attraction to my father and, as I grew older, to me. He knew their owners well, as during the winter they often sent their engines to our works in Bell Lane for overhaul and he would spend some time talking to them and the drivers most of whom he knew by their Christian names. There were the Beeches, Birds, Grays, Irvings, Pettigroves, and other famous fairground families, and they all knew that my father would help them out if their engines needed attention when they were in our area.

A Fairground scene in the Chilterns circa 1926.

On Sunday morning when the fair was being dismantled it was quite a different scene that met our eyes as we approached and entered the town in our horse and trap or motor car as the case happened to be. We always went to Amersham on Sundays as my father was a devout man and attended a small meeting of Christians in the high street each week. He brought me up to have a faith in God which I am thankful to say has remained firm throughout my long and eventful life.

After settling our horse in the stables at The Crown hostelry under the watchful eye of the ancient white Cockatoo which presided there at that time, we made our way through the street and were fascinated by the skill and expertise of the fair ground people as they dismantled their equipment ready to move off. The drivers of the showmen's engines, some of which were equipped with cranes, lent a hand to load heavy equipment on to specially built trailers and eventually manoeuvred them into position, coupling them to the living vans ready to tow away a string of five, six or more vehicles. In due course they ponderously steamed away through the beautiful Chiltern Hills to their next port of call.

Not all the fairs were as large or as important as Amersham and throughout the summer village events were staged on a small scale. I recall visiting such a fair in the Chilterns with my father when I was a young boy. He had been called in to deal with some engineering problem by Mrs. Bird. We were invited into her ornate caravan to discuss the business and I remember that throughout the talks the good lady kept a sharp watch on the steam roundabout which was positioned in her line of vision. Her mind must have worked like a computer as she counted the number of riders and calculated the takings to a penny. Woe betide the attendant if he did not turn in the exact amount due.

Fowler three speed showman's engine near Chesham Circa 1910. Photo author's collection.

From time to time showman's engines would pass along the main Hatfield to Reading road and the crews would stop for a drink at the White Lion public house at the top of Bell Lane. There was comparatively little traffic in those days and not much noise, so we could hear the engines coming from up to a mile or more away. Certainly as they rounded the corner at the sheep houses approaching Chalfont Road Station we could pick up the sound and follow their progress.

I well remember on one autumn evening listening to the approach of two such engines. From the ringing of the gearing my brother and I who were both young boys surmised that they were Burrells and we were quite right. It was twilight by the time that they reached the White Lion and stopped. One of the showmen hurried down to our works and asked for our help. He explained that they were running later than expected, were on their way to Prestwood Fair and that they had no lights. Could we lend him some engine lamps until the following day when, he promised, hand on heart, that he would return them?

My father was probably away at the time because I recall that we took the man to our lamp store and let him have two sets of our well trimmed and filled oil lamps. We were so naive and trusting that we sent him off without enquiring his name or getting a receipt. Regrettably our faith in human nature was shattered as we never saw the showman or our lamps again. My father was none too pleased with us but we did not make the same mistake again and it taught us an important lesson in business practice.

Burrell Showman's engine at a country fair in the Chilterns 1920s.

When I was about seven years old a fund-raising fair for charity was held in the Park at Beel House and two fine showman's engines arrived together with a steam driven roundabout and other associated equipment and stalls. Although I was too young to know much about engines I now realise that one engine was a Burrell and I suspect that it was nearly new. It was beautifully kept and I remember noticing that even the injector was highly polished.

In spite of my tender years my mother gave me sixpence to spend and I was allowed to visit the fair during the afternoon on my own. It was a lovely day and after admiring the engines I took a ride on the steam roundabout. Later I noticed a stall attended by a pretty girl and decided to try my hand at winning a prize. By some remarkable chance I won a large, ornate, but quite useless, gaudy glass ornament with my first throw much to the consternation of the attendant, who I feel sure had quite wrongly assumed that she had arranged the stall in such a way as to make it almost impossible to win anything except the smallest of articles.

She was quite put out and offered me half a crown if I would sell the ornament back to her but I would not agree as I wanted to give it to my mother. I hurried home with my prize and my gracious parent was touched that I had won it for her. I thought no more of the incident until many years later after her death when I was equally moved to find the ornament carefully stored away with her best bone china.

Fowler "Supreme" Owner Mr. Jack Wharton, Witney, Oxon.

"Supreme" was the last Fowler Showman's engine to be made and was supplied new in 1934. After serving for some years on the showgrounds she was sold to Scotland where she was used to haul large railway locomotives to the docks for export. Mr. Jack Wharton of Witney carried out a superlative job when he purchased the engine, painstakingly rebuilding and restoring it to its former glory.

As I grew up my interest in showman's engines was maintained and in my travels I always kept an eye open for them. I remember seeing a well maintained Foster belonging to Thurston's generating electricity on Newmarket Heath one evening after dark. The driver was friendly, inviting me on to the footplate. The engine was working hard, running well, and apart from a slight flexing of the horn plate when the boiler feed pump was applied I could not fault it in any way. It was an unforgettable experience.

When moving from place to place, a large set of fair ground paraphernalia was a sight to behold. I remember seeing four showman's engines in convoy passing through Farnham Surrey before the war. Each engine hauled a long string of trailers and even in those days when traffic was light compared with present day conditions the outfit caused quite a tail back of impatient road users as the engines rattled proudly through the town. For my part the sight more than compensated for any inconvenience caused by the cavalcade.

Chapter VII

EASTERN COUNTIES

Burrell Ploughing Engine Number 767 cultivating at Walton-on-Naze Essex in the early 1920's Driver Banks, Owner J W Eagle.

Our holidays were invariably spent in the Eastern Counties and during the course of many years we came to know the coast and hinterland from Lincolnshire to South East Essex quite well. My father liked the area around Frinton, Walton-on-the-Naze and Clacton, and had many friends there, so we often made our base in that region. Sailing , swimming and beach games occupied much of our time but there were other distractions. We enjoyed the half dozen or so "Belle" coal fired steam paddle pleasure steamers plying between London and Yarmouth calling at all the piers as they went. The ill fated "Crested Eagle" paddle steamer also provided trips from Clacton and my friend Peter St. John and I were thrilled to sail to Calais and back on her when we were young boys. Alas she was bombed and sunk a decade later whilst helping to rescue the army from Dunkirk.

However our main hobby was tracking and photographing the hundreds of agricultural traction engines in East Anglia. As we took our holidays in late August and early September most of them were at work dealing with after-harvest activities. Steam ploughing and cultivating had not yet been replaced by the internal or "infernal" combustion engine as my father preferred to call it, and there were dozens of fine sets, many of them quite or almost new, breaking up the stubble and preparing the land for sowing. On farms everywhere threshing by steam was in full swing and the farmers were friendly. As long as we observed normal courtesies, did not leave gates open or contravene the codes of countryside behaviour, which as countrymen ourselves we respected in any case, we went more or less wherever we wanted as we tracked down our quarry.

33

Savage Sandringham Class engine driving Holmes thresher near Buckingham Green, Norfolk circa 1929 Owner Loveday.

The variety of makes and types of engines and associated equipment was wide. There were over forty makers in the United Kingdom, and many were bult in the Eastern Counties. Some were old and some new, the older the better as far as our hobby was concerned and we were always on the look out for rare species and specimens. The wheels on the threshing and steam ploughing tackle were steel shod, and they left marks on the roads. These marks supplemented by other clues, such as damp patches where the boiler feed injectors had "slobbered" or tell-tale signs where the engines had picked up water at streams or ponds made it possible for us to assess when an engine had passed that way as we tracked them down like Red Indians on the war path.

Inevitably some finds were more important than others and often, after following the tracks for some miles, we would come upon yet another Single Crank Compound Burrell built at Thetford, Norfolk. These were fine and very popular engines, hence the large numbers in use, but they were so plentiful that we did not always stop to photograph them. One evening in late summer as we followed a lead given to us by an engineman we cautiously reconnoited the village of Buckingham Green, Norfolk. We had heard that there were Savages on the green and we were taking no chances. So, with camera cocked we crept forward, in single file, towards some buildings under a clump of trees. Quite suddenly we came upon our quarry and were surrounded by them. Fortunately they were harmless as they were not in steam. They were all single cylinder, and had all been built at Kings Lynn, Norfolk, and were very rare.

Allchin Engine threshing near Kenninghall Norfolk Circa 1929. Owner Loveday
T.T.B. on left (in Trilby) talks to the owner's brother (in bowler).

Their owner, Mr. Loveday, who was one of the old school and wore a bowler hat, proved to be very friendly and it soon became clear that my father had found a man with a "kindred spirit". We were told that if we returned a few days later, provided the weather held fine, we could see some of the engines and tackle at work threshing from the "stook", or in other words threshing directly from the field before the sheaves were built into ricks.

He carried out the maintenance of his machines himself and showed us the equipment with which he bored out the cylinders on his engines. The bearings on the shakers of his threshing machines were also home made. He had a theory that chilled cast iron bearings created less friction than the normal brass, as used by most makers at that time.

The opportunity to see the engines at work was not to be missed, as not only were the engines rare and locally made but the threshing machines were even more rare, having been built by Holmes of Norwich. Every other thresher that we had ever seen had the corn spouts at the rear of the machine; these were different, they had the spouts at the side. Even at that time they were almost an extinct species. Alas shortly afterwards they were exterminated and gone for ever. Mr. Loveday took us to see some of his engines at work in the late summer harvest fields of the delightful Norfolk countryside. He also took us to Kenninghall to visit his brother whose engines included a Holmes, probably the last to exist, and an unusual Allchin, threshing in the mellow evening light hard by a fine old windmill which still had its sails intact.

Garrett Overtype Steam Tipping Wagon (Note the belt driven tipping gear) at our Bell Lane Works circa 1929, when in the ownership of T.T.B. Driver Harold Hearn.

In the heyday of the industrial revolution there were at least fourteen makers of traction and portable steam engines in the Eastern Counties, of which four were in Lincoln. As we travelled on our hunting trips we found examples of all these makes as well as many others built in other parts of England.

Many of the works where the engines were made were still active in the 1920's and my father was able to arrange for us to visit two of them. As a potential customer he was made welcome and we were well received.

The first works that we visited were Garrett's of Leiston, Suffolk. We were on holiday near Dunwich during the summer school holidays of 1927 and my father decided to take up an invitation to visit the plant as it was not far from where we were staying. Among his fleet of steam waggons he had a Garrett overtype and the makers were trying to persuade him to replace it with one of their undertype "Longdogs", hence the invitation. Work was scarce for makers of agricultural machinery at that period between the wars and many of the shops that formerly made threshing machines were deserted. There were however, compensations for us as the "Longdogs" were being built and we found some of the manufacturing processes of particular interest, especially the large hydraulic press that was forming the main frames for the waggons. We also witnessed drop forging which was new to us and were impressed with the whole scale of the works which was much larger than our operation at Amersham at that time.

Garrett Suffolk Punch Timber Tractor passing through Braintree Essex Circa 1931 when in the ownership of John Sadd of Maldon.

Three years later we returned to Leiston and saw one of their "Suffolk Punch" steam timber-hauling tractors on test hauling two heavily laden "Longdogs" through the town. The stoker on these tractors was separated from the driver by the boiler and had his own compartment in the rear which was rather an unusual and I thought awkward arrangement.

During the Commercial Motor Show at Olympia some time later we saw one of the same tractors on display. It was surrounded by rocks and rubber plants and looked really impressive but they only built three, of which, one was exported to South Africa and two were sold to John Sadd of Maldon, Essex.

The other works that we toured were Ransomes Sims & Jefferies' at Ipswich. Like Garretts they were in the doldrums in some traditional departments but, having diversified, were busy in others. They were making Electric Trolley buses for use on the streets of Ipswich as well as a wide range of domestic lawn mowers. They were also producing agricultural ploughs and implements in large quantities.

Ransomes had been building steam engines for nearly ninety years and we were fortunate enough to see the final batch of traction engines being completed and tested. They were the last of a long line and it was the end of an era.

I have since learnt that some of the batch which we saw never found a customer and were sadly scrapped without ever leaving the works.

Chapter VIII

BLACK JACK

*   *   *   *   *   *   *   *   *   *   *   *   *   *   *   *

"Black Jack" leading the procession through Reading celebrating Queen Victoria's Diamond Jubilee 1897.

Black Jack had his twenty first birthday the year that I was born. It is not recorded that there were any special celebrations to mark his coming of age which is understandable as it was war time. He always enjoyed a special place in my father's affections as he had been acquired to head a dynasty of traction engines when our business was founded in 1897.

There is no doubt that Black Jack is an extrovert and you could say that he is more than a little big headed. He certainly has the largest chimney of any threshing engine that I know. He is a chauvinistic male. Whereas most steam engines were referred to as "She", Black Jack is invariably alluded to as "He".

The circumstances of his birth may be partially responsible for his character but there are probably other factors as well. A brief study of his life history may help us to discover why he is what he is.

First of all he is a Fowler which in the opinion of many makes him an aristocrat of the traction engine world. Furthermore he is no "run of the mill" product from the famous Leeds stable. He came into the world predestined to represent his makers at the Royal Counties Show held at Reading in 1897. Consequently particular care was taken in his manufacture and when he first appeared well manicured and made up to show finish standards he was the "creme de la creme".

"Black Jack" threshing near Amersham, Bucks. Circa 1929 . Owner T.T.B., Driver George Ruff.

This was no ordinary occasion; it was Queen Victoria's Diamond Jubilee Year; the British Empire was at its peak, and celebrations were the order of the day. There were seventy or so engines at the show and makers were vying with each other as they extolled the virtues of their prodigies.

Tom Boughton, accompanied by his father who had offered to buy him a new engine to start him in business, went from stand to stand in his search of the best example on display. After much thought, deliberation, and advice he chose and purchased Black Jack. At the close of the show the proud engine, bedecked with flags and banners led the Jubilee procession through Reading. It was enough to turn any engine's head.

Later he steamed to his new home driven by the venerable George Harris, a driver of no mean repute. A man carrying a red flag walked before to herald his approach, an honour accorded to few of us. His new owner lived in a fine old and historic manor house of great charm at Chenies, Buckinghamshire which may have impressed him. It is not recorded that he showed any emotion when he arrived but the experience may have left its mark.

He settled down well and worked hard turning his hand to threshing, hauling, sawing, pumping and other duties made necessary by the absence of motor cars, trucks, combine harvesters and other accoutrements of later years. He even stood in for a showman's engine on one occasion, and drove the dynamo generating electricity to power the rides and music at a local fair whilst repairs were carried out to the ornate Foster road locomotive which normally did the work.

In 1921 an event occurred which probably boosted his self confidence. His owner decided to re-organise his business and sell some of his agricultural machinery. An auction sale was arranged and twelve sets of threshing tackle together with a set of steam ploughing engines were lined up to go under the hammer.

Black Jack was the last in the line and bidding commenced. Tom watched and felt a lump coming into his throat. The strain of parting with a faithful friend was too much for him so he took up the bidding and saved the engine for posterity. He has remained in the family ownership ever since.

His working life continued for thirty years after the sale before he went into retirement. He has always enjoyed excellent health and has led a charmed life. Casualties among traction engines were murderously heavy around the time that he retired and hundreds of fine engines came under the searing torture of the cutting torch.

Line up at auction sale of surplus plant by T.T.B. 1921.

"Black Jack" taking part in the Lord Mayor's Show in the City of London 1978.
Owner Mr. Trafford Boughton.

Not only has Black Jack survived but due to some highly skilled surgery, he is in excellent physical shape. Partly out of affection for him but more in honour of his later owner, the family arranged for the eminent boiler surgeon Walter Gower of Bedford to carry out a fire-box and boiler barrel transplant. The operation was a complete success and although the effects of advancing years cannot be entirely eradicated, he is in most respects as good as new.

In the autumn of his life he revels in the high life and adores Show Business. He loses no opportunity to attend Rallies, Carnivals, Fetes, Weddings and Road Runs. In the 1970s he was even an honoured guest at the Lord Mayor's Show in London where he hauled a trailer on which was mounted a Rolls Royce Aero engine reputed to be worth £1,000,000. Keeping in step with crack military regiments, he marched through the city as though to the manner born. He has no vicious habits if treated with care, although he is rather hasty when his blood pressure is high and he is blowing his top. He drinks but not to excess, and enjoys a quiet smoke.

No history of Black Jack would be complete without reference to the many generations of fine retainers who tended and cared for him throughout his long life: Dickie Groom, the Harrises, Hearns, Lockes, Ratcliffes and Ruffs and many others to whom Black Jack and the Boughton family owe a debt of gratitude.

*   *   *   *   *   *   *   *   *   *   *   *   *   *   *   *

Chapter IX

THE YARD

Fowler Three Speed Road Locomotive on military service passing through Sir Lowry's pass, Hottentot Holland Mountains, South Africa Circa 1900. Photo Author's collection

For many years the premises which have developed into the "Boughton" Works in Bell Lane were known by all those who worked for my father as the "Yard". If it had not been for the South African or Boer War, it is unlikely that it would have developed in the way that it did and it would probably have remained a depot to which engines and plant returned between jobs.

As we have seen, my father started his business by buying a brand new traction engine, Black Jack, which would not require any major repairs for many years. After he had been established for two years or so, he saw the need for a second engine and ordered another Fowler identical to the first. However, the Boer War broke out and the makers works at Leeds was required to support the war effort by increasing the production of three-speed compound Road Locomotives needed to haul guns and supplies in South Africa. Accordingly they were unable to supply my father with his second engine and he decided to buy a second-hand Aveling and Porter instead.

The Aveling had seen many years of service and had been used, among other things, to haul materials for the building of the Rothschild Mansion at Waddesden. It had a very large boiler barrel, a single speed road gear, and no differential between the rear wheels. By comparison with the modern "Black Jack", the Aveling was antiquated and old fashioned, and it was not long before the drivers christened it "Granny".

"Granny" threshing near Chalfont St. Peter Circa 1927. Tom Boughton with back to camera taking notes.

Inevitably, in due course, "Granny" and other second hand engines purchased subsequently, needed major repairs including new fire-boxes. My father decided to carry out the work himself aided by boiler-makers whom he hired from Allchin's of Northampton or Fowler of Leeds.

He then embarked on a policy of recruiting his own team of skilled people and equipped his works to maintain and re-build his own engines and those of other steam engine users in the district. His reputation grew and in due course, he became involved with the installation and maintenance of power plants in factories, brick-works, saw mills and laundries over a wide area. In addition he attended to his own fleet of steam powered plant which continually increased in size. It was always a thrill to me when the local show-men sent their elite engines in for repairs, especially in the early days before the recession when they were kept in immaculate, highly polished condition, regardless of cost.

In order to keep his cash flow positive and his men gainfully employed throughout the year he adapted some of his traction engines and made them convertible into steam rollers. They could then be used in the winter for threshing and during other seasons could be hired out to repair the roads. He also purchased a number of light steam haulage tractors and converted them into rollers as well. His great friend Harry Shepherd of Luton assisted him with the design and innovation called for in this work.

43

Tasker "Little Giant" 1676. Hauling a large barge used to float a steam grab to excavate gravel in the Colne Valley near Rickmansworth, Herts. Driver Sydney Radcliffe. Owner T.T.B.

Among his many business interests were a brick works and sand pits at Porridge Pot, Linslade near Leighton Buzzard in which he was a major share holder. He invested in these enterprises in order to ensure work for his steam wagons. He also ran steam saw-mills which in turn provided work for haulage engines and tractors. As well as hauling for his own mills he provided a service to other timber users and merchants including Herbert Groves, a great friend and supporter over many years.

Indivisible loads of large proportions were frequently hauled including complete gravel excavating plants comprising barges, steam diggers and associated equipment from one site to another as pits become exhausted and new diggings were found in the Colne Valley. Lakes and water sport facilities stretching from Bushey to Denham still bear witness to these massive operations. The barges were built by Walkers of Rickmansworth and were hauled by road to the sites by my father's "Little Giants". There was just enough room to get a large barge through Watford High Street provided all the shop blinds were closed. These operations were usually carried out at night or very early in the morning when there was little traffic about and the whole operation was supervised by the police with whom my father always tried to maintain good relations. The "entente cordiale" was marred from time to time when the engines were reported for making too much smoke or by being involved in some misdemeanour but by and large the authorities were co-operative.

BEFORE THEIR SEPARATION AT THE WHIPSNADE "ZOO": "DIXIE" AND "ROSIE," OF BOSTOCK'S TRAVELLING MENAGERIE FAME, ON THEIR ARRIVAL AT DUNSTABLE STATION FROM GLASGOW.

Animals arriving at Dunstable station from Glasgow January 1932.

Haulage of all kinds was undertaken including the heavy sector involving large indivisible and unusual loads. The L.M.S. railway company contracted with my father to handle heavy goods of all sorts from the point of arrival at railway stations to their ultimate destination. This contract led to some unusual assignments, one of the most interesting of which was the transportation of circus animals from Dunstable station to Whipsnade around the time that the famous zoo was formed.

Information reached my father during January 1931 that a large consignment of special trailers containing circus animals was due to arrive at Dunstable station at a precise time one Monday morning. My father was required to provide motive power to haul the trailers from the station to the new zoo situated high up on the Dunstable Downs.

Accordingly he despatched two of his Tasker "Little Giant" steam tractors driven by Sidney Ratcliffe and "John Henry" Kaley to meet the train that had travelled all the way down from Scotland. It transpired that the animals had formed part of the famous Bostock & Wombwell's Menagerie and had been sold to the London Zoo which owned Whipsnade.

45

Burrell Showman's engine "Nero" purchased new by Bostock & Wombwell to haul their menagerie.
Photo shows "Nero" happily in preservation at Weeting rally 1989.

Although the "Little Giants" were smaller than the fine Burrell Showmen's engines "RAJAH" and "NERO" that had been used by the circus owners when travelling the country, they performed manfully and hauled the heavy loads safely up the long hills to their destination.

On arrival at the site, due to soft ground conditions, difficulties arose in placing the trailers exactly where the authorities wanted them to be. My father who was pondering what to do next was surprised to see one of the vehicles moving forward as though of its own accord. Upon investigation he discovered that the keepers had called on the elephant (Dixie) to lend a hand, or rather a head, to push the trailers as it had been trained to do whenever the circus was on the move. The trailers had in fact been reinforced for this very purpose.

A film of the operation was made at the time which created a great deal of interest when it appeared on many of the newsreels at local cinemas.

A Group of Boughton Employees in the early 1920s . From the left: George Hearn, (Nipper); Amos Rixon, Unknown; Lew Pearce; Alf Scott; Arch Hawkes (Founder of Mayo & Hawkes, Cycle Dealers, Chesham 1928); Charlie Hoar and (Mr.) Todd on far right.

For many of those formative years the works was in the charge of Lew Pearce whom my father had recruited from Warminster in Wiltshire. Lew had many attributes and was skilled in a wide variety of facets of practical engineering including foundry practices. He brought with him a new dimension of experience and expertise which was a great benefit to the business. His son Harold, who worked under his father, was a good friend to my brother and me and we watched many a fine game of Rugby-football together on Saturday afternoons in a field behind the Pineapple public house. Lew's younger brother Jack, a war-wounded veteran from World War One drove engines for the firm until he retired. All the Pearces had a keen sense of humour which made working with them a pleasure. They were constantly ragged about being Wilshire Moonrakers but they took it all in good part.

Jack often recounted how, on one occasion, during the 1914-18 war he was marching up to the front line when a young officer who had become separated from his unit called out "Are you the West Riding"?; to which he replied "No; we are the Wilts .... walking".

The Yard was the scene of constant activity as many engines were based there and quite a few of those engaged in road transport returned every evening to be refuelled and watered ready for an early start the following morning. At five o'clock in the morning the works carpenter, Alf Scott, arrived to light the fires in the waggons and tractors so that by the time the drivers arrived the engines had a head of steam and once they were oiled round they could move off without delay.

Early days at The Yard with Tom Boughton (fifth from left) and his team carrying out major surgery to his engines. Foreman George Harris (wielding sledge hammer) third from left.

On dark winter mornings the glow from the ash-pans of the engines sent out shafts of light as they passed our house and I still clearly remember the hissing sound of the drain cocks as the drivers cleared the condensate from the cylinders before changing into top gear and headed for the open road.

Most of my father's engines were painted the same colour, Mid Brunswick Green, and were lined out in light green and yellow. They were normally refurbished when they came in for major overhauls and the painting was carried out by Aubrey Barden, a sterling character who had lost a leg above the knee whilst serving on the Western Front during 1918. He was a very brave man and flatly refused to allow his disability to affect his work adversely.

He had his bicycle specially adapted with a fixed wheel which enabled him to use his good leg to pedal from Chenies to the works, come hail, rain or shine. Painting, lining out, and sign writing were all skills that he acquired but he was also an expert tree-feller and carpenter.

On the dot of seven o'clock every morning a hand bell pealed out summoning all employees to attend and "clock-on". The bell was wielded in the manner reminiscent of a town cryer by Fred Hyde who like Aubrey had lost a leg in battle. As a war-wounded veteran he had been trained in the art of book keeping under a government scheme and, as he often joked, his instructor had instilled into him, "if you are not busy; ... look busy".

Clayton & Shuttleworth 40691 hauling contractor's locomotive used on the construction of the Watford by-pass 1920s. Driver E Burgin. Owner T.T.B.

Fred was in sole charge of the office and accordingly had a wide variety of duties from invoicing to paying the wages and keeping the books. He collected the money from the Bank and dealt with the customers and employees. He ordered supplies and took as much credit as possible from suppliers. He kept his cool and I cannot remember ever seeing him angry.

He worked at a high-topped desk of which Scrooge would have approved, and sat on a high stool (of which he would not). In spite of his disability he developed a technique which enabled him to swing on to the stool with considerable agility, a feat which most able-bodied men would have found difficult to emulate. He followed his training meticulously and was never still for a moment as he sporadically reached out for ledgers and books between answering the telephone and typing letters.

His means of transport was a belt-driven Rudge Multi motor-cycle with infinitely variable speeds. He used this steed to travel to work and also to visit recalcitrant slow-paying customers in attempts to extract payment of outstanding debts due to the firm. On more than one occasion some of the more militant farmers threatened to punch his nose or even throw him down a well if he persisted in his quest, but he was not easily deviated from his purpose and usually came away with something on account without prejudicing future business. He did a fine job and was trusted implicitly.

Fowler Steam Ploughing Engine at Pond Park, Chesham ready to pull waggons loaded with building materials up to the top of Addison Road. Driver Will Harris. Owner T.T.B.

Innovation and problem-solving were the pursuits that my father most enjoyed and the business grew as a result. He undertook the most unlikely tasks often for the sheer pleasure of helping someone out or of accepting a challenge which others did not want to solve. On one occasion a large barge containing a heavy steam gravel-digging grab sank in deep water in the Colne Valley. The owner made a number of unsuccessful attempts to re-float it and at last called in my father. By the ingenious use of two of his heavy winching tractors harnessed to multiple rope pulleys, the operation, under the astute guidance of the experienced Dickie Groom, was accomplished, and the barge which weighed at least fifty tons was salvaged. The whole operation had taken less than two days.

When the Pond Park housing estate was being built at Chesham in the late 1920s, the vehicles delivering the materials could not climb the steep Addison Road at the top of which the estate was constructed. Even the Sentinel steam waggons belonging to Wood and Whittaker of Wendover failed to master the hill. Tom Boughton was asked for his advice and help. He solved the problem by positioning a steam ploughing engine at a strategic point and winching the loaded waggons up the hill. The empty waggons took the rope down as they left. The solution worked like a charm. The same system was used during World War Two to assist the Tasker "Little Giant" climb the steep hill with timber from Sarratt Bottom for the "Rifle Butt Contract". On another occasion he undertook to move a complete wooden-framed granary by road and even moved a grocer's shop together with its contents in situ without mishap.

50

Chapter X

FODEN'S BRAVE ATTEMPT
TO CHECK THE INCOMING TIDE OF DIESEL

Foden "Speed Six" . Photo courtesy of Mr. S Satterthwaite

As the 1920s drew to a close, the makers and users of Steam waggons were coming under increasing competition from Diesel and petrol-driven trucks. "The writing was on the wall" for all to interpret as best they could. In fact the steam waggon era was nearing its end, but a core of die-hards steadfastly refused to accept the inevitable, with the result that considerable sums were expended on research and development of steam transport by a number of makers engaged in battles reminiscent of "Custer's last stand". Many users remained loyal to steam for a long time and it was not until well into the 1950's that the last pockets of resistance capitulated. Liverpool held out to the bitter end as did a few operators of tar spraying and other specialised equipment. Even then many steam waggons passed into the preservation movement and are still the pride and joy of their owners and crews.

Foden Speed Six being demonstrated in South Africa Circa 1931
Photo courtesy Mr. S. Satterthwaite on left of picture.

It was probably during the autumn of 1929 that I saw a "Speed Six" for the first time. I was a school boy then and my father took my brother and me to the Commercial Motor show in London. I think that it was held in Olympia but I cannot be sure of the venue after the lapse of so many years.

What I can remember vividly however, is my first sight of the "Speed Six" posed in its best show livery preening itself on Foden's stand. Having been brought up accustomed to the sight of my father's working waggons in every day use, I knew something of the problems facing the best of crews as they stove to keep their waggons, in which they took a great pride, smart, clean and efficient.

Foden "Speed Twelve" belonging to Murrell's Wharf.

Here at the exhibition was something quite new to me: a brand new steam waggon of revolutionary design and concept, presented with panache and professionalism. The burnished brass fittings and gleaming copper pipes complemented by a paint finish that would have done credit to a coach in the royal mews, combined to make it a sight to behold. There was not a speck of coal or any other dust anywhere and the cab both inside and out was unstained by fumes or smoke.

My father who was never overfond of internal combustion engines, admired the waggon and told us that he thought Fodens had come up with the answer to the threat from the diesel engine. He liked the unobstructed view from the drivers position, the high pressure superheated steam, the totally enclosed engine, the steam brakes, the shaft drive and the pneumatic tyres. These features contrasted with those of his overtype waggons, all of which were on solid tyres.

After the show "Speed Six" and "Speed Twelve" waggons began to appear on the roads and as we travelled we were always on the look out for them. Some of the Murrell's Wharf fleet came out from London in our direction from time to time and others could be seen further afield. I remember seeing a "Speed Six" near Winchester hauling pig and poultry food and a "Speed Twelve" passing through Slough with a cargo of roofing tiles.

Foden Overtype Converted from a six wheeled tipper to a Timber Tractor with Steam Winch behind the cab.
It was later converted to pneumatic tyres all round. Six waggons were converted in this way.
Driver Harold Hearn, Owner T.T.B.

The nearest to us belonged to T. Leigh de Fraine of Chartridge near Chesham, a young man who had learnt his trade under the auspices of my father. Leigh operated a number of overtype waggons and an "E" type Foden undertype but he complained that the latter used too much coal and exchanged it for a new "Speed Twelve".

He often drove the waggon himself hauling bricks from Calvert, but he did not keep it long as the road tax was high and the legal carrying capacity, especially when fully coaled and watered up, was lower than he thought was economical and profitable. Furthermore, in addition to the driver he needed a stoker, which entailed extra expense, so he exchanged it for two diesels which Fodens had started to produce instead of steam in or about 1932.

Foden Overtype Timber Tractor KX 5003 unloading trees at Woodrow Sawmill near Amersham Circa 1939. Driver A.G. Kayley (John Henry) . Owner T.T.B.

At that time my father was operating a number of overtype tractors and trailers of various makes in addition to some steam waggons, rollers and traction engines. The tractors were used to haul trees to feed the many saw mills in the area particularly in High Wycombe, Chesham, Berkhamsted and elsewhere. They did a good job but they had a limited range. The road tax on tractors was lower than on waggons so it made sense to convert waggons into tractors, an exercise which my father and brother proceeded to carry out by shortening the wheelbase on the waggons and fitting winches behind the cabs. These were powered by twin cylinder steam launch engines supplied by steam from the waggon boiler and were very successful.

Competition in the early 1930s was rife and we were all looking for better equpment. It was a time of transition and steam was still widely used. Harold Judd of Spencers Wood near Reading bought a new "Sentinel" steam timber tractor (Old Bill) on pneumatic tyres and my father cast around for some way of going one better. He hit on the idea that a "Speed Six" shortened and converted into a tractor with one of his steam winches would be the solution to the problem.

Foden Overtype KX 5003 hauling large load through Leighton Buzzard Circa 1938.
Driver A.G. Kaley (John Henry) Owner T.T.B.

It so happened that one came on to the market second-hand and was advertised in the trade journals of the time. My father answered the advertisement and took my brother and me to Kidlington near Oxford to see it. On arrival we met the owner, Mr. Partridge and his dog, which followed him wherever he went and seemed to take a great interest in everything his master said. Together they showed us the "Speed Six" number 14044 which he had for sale. In addition he had two other tippers of the same make and type which were in steam hauling gravel from his pit. It was an impressive sight watching the heavily loaded waggons and trailers climbing the steep slope from the pit bottom.

Mr. Partridge had already shortened number 14044 as he had intended to use it as a tractor to take advantage of lower road taxes but had changed his mind. The work that he had carried out suited us for the business and my father made an offer, which, ofter consulting with his dog, Mr. Partridge accepted. We were at last the proud owners of one of the last few "Speed Sixes" to be built and although it was not in such pristine condition as the one which we had seen at Olympia a few years earlier, we were well pleased.

Foden "Speed Six" 14044 Converted to Timber Tractor, hauling trees near Watford Circa 1936.
Driver Alf Hearn on left. Sonny Knowles on his left and D. Lee in Cab. Owner T.T.B.

A few days later I accompanied my brother, who was to drive the "Speed Six" home, to Kidlington and after appropriate preparations steamed away, watched by Mr. Partridge and his dog. Apart from a scare when we ran short of water crossing the Chiltern escarpment near Wendover, all went well and we duly reached Amersham safely.

The tractor was overhauled in our works and a winch driven by a twin cylinder steam launch engine built by Seekings of Gloucester in 1883 was installed. Streamlined water tanks similar to those on Harold Judd's Sentinel were also made and long range coal bunkers were fitted. Painted in dark green and sign-written with yellow and black lettering the "Speed Six" looked really smart and we were very proud of it.

For a time all went well and the tractor hauling a six-wheeled pole waggon, which we had built using the rear bogie from a Garrett Long Dog six-wheeled steam waggon, travelled far and wide delivering trees to Birmingham and other destinations throughout the Midlands and Southern Counties.

Alas, like all good things, this period of successful operation came to an end, and one evening our driver, Alf Hean, reported a wisp of steam escaping from a location just above the foundation ring, and upon close inspection an ominous crack was diagnosed.

Foden "Speed Six" Timber Tractor converted from tipper hauling trees Circa 1936
Driver Alf Hearn, Owner T.T.B.

This discovery posed a serious dilemma. The pistol-shaped, all-welded No. 2 boilers of the type fitted to our vehicle were not popular with insurance companies at the best of times and we realised that they would not permit us to weld a crack in the boiler shell. We did not want to scrap our tractor and we could not locate a boiler like ours. Fodens had by this time ceased making steamers so that we could not buy a new one.

The thought of fitting a Sentinel boiler sprang to our minds and we surmised that if such a boiler provided enough steam to propel one make of waggon it would do the same for another. True, the heating surface on the "Speed Six" was greater than on the Sentinel but the grate area on the latter was larger so we took the view that the odds were that such an installation would work out satisfactorily. Furthermore, we knew that our friend Frank Prentice of Tring had a good, little used, Sentinel boiler so we decided to proceed.

Unfortunately, as Robbie Burns reminds us "The best laid plans of mice and men gang aft aglee" and the conversion was almost a complete failure. In spite of many experiments with exhaust nozzles and varying lengths of chimney the result was a disaster. When we reduced the draught the boiler would not generate sufficient steam and when it was increased the consumption of fuel was excessive and uneconomic. There was no acceptable happy medium. It was a no win situation.

Allchin six Ton Steam Waggon converted to Timber Tractor hauling trees near Tring, Herts. Circa 1934. Driver A.K. Kaley (John Henry) Owner T.T.B.

There was nothing for it but to abandon our "Speed Six" and it was a sad day when it came under the brutal attention of the acetylene burner. Until we could get a replacement our overtypes took the strain, often manned by shift crews working round the clock. Eventually the tide of change was too strong to resist and like King Canute we had to concede defeat as we switched from steam to diesel. Happily six of our Foden overtypes survived to the preservation era and are safely in the hands of dedicated enthusiasts, so the spirit of steam lives on.

Chapter XI

A TENDER PLANT

Brown & May Tractor re-built with light weight wide wheels to make it suitable for consolidating in-fill on the Great West Road renewal programme at Brentford in the 1920s. Owner T.T.B..The contractors used a steam locomotive named "Brill" which they had acquired from the Brill Tramway near Aylesbury, to cart the spoil from the steam digger to the embankment on which the Brown & May was working.

It was early in the new year of 1935 that I started in the business. Getting up ready to report for duty at seven o'clock on a cold winter's morning, in a works with no heating to speak of, was quite a cultural shock. The men used to "buffet" to keep warm and I have no doubt that I did the same.

There was much to learn, and for the first two years I absorbed as much knowledge as possible in the skills of engineering especially as they applied to the repairs and rebuilding of steam engines and related plant. Being the Boss's son did not insulate me from the round of practical jokes which are traditionally reserved for new-comers, trainees and apprentices to engineering, and I found myself visiting the stores to collect sky hooks, wimwoms for a goose's bridle and other non-existent articles, as generations have done before and since.

As time went on, and as soon as I was old enough, I took a driving test that had been introduced that very year. From time to time I was sent on assignments away from the works which made a welcome diversion. On one occasion, I drove Lew Pearce to Exeter to repair our Aveling roller 4804 which was working on the by-pass at Countess Weir, Devon.

Group clearing trees in Chesham Park. Dickie Groom in centre of picture with Ted Burgin on his right and George Adams on his left. Frank Honey by the door of the Foden. Owner T.T.B.

The business was going through a period of change, something which seems to be the story of my life, as progress has no time for the "status quo". The method of making roads had changed, and concrete had largely taken over from water and tarmacadam. This change dramatically reduced the demand for steam rollers and posed problems as to the direction that the business should take.

It is said that when one door closes another opens, and although there is no guarantee that this will happen, I have found that there are windows or doors of opportunity ready to be opened by those who have the vision to recognise them.

So it was at that time. The demand for housing was insatiable just as it is today, and London was sprawling out in all directions like lava from an erupting volcano. Land had to be cleared of trees to make room for new suburbs and building estates. This type of work was ideal as the age of the Bull-Dozer had not dawned and the traction engine was still king. Besides, trees were needed for the saw mills.

In order to learn the business, I spent time in various areas of activity, not always in the works, but on the operational sites. I gravitated towards the agricultural contracting side of our activities and following on the years of engine-spotting, lost no opportunities to drive the traction engines. Threshing and steam ploughing were the occupations that I liked most of all. Whilst I was still in my teens I became competent to take charge of a threshing set on my own although I had to be accompanied by a licenced steersman until I was twenty-one when I was granted a licence for all groups.

Fowler "Central" involved in an accident at White Hill Chesham, late 1890s. Owner T.T.B.

Operating a steam threshing set is like many other occupations, quite straight forward when you know how, but full of pitfalls whilst you are learning and gaining experience. It is one thing to climb on to an engine in a rally field and take it round the arena; it is another to line it up to a threshing machine in a wet and soggy field in the middle of winter especially if you have to line up a baler or chaff-cutter to the machine as well. It is even more difficult to get a good day's output out of the set and to satisfy a crusty farmer three times your own age. Negotiating steep hills can also be tricky.

Having prepared the outfit for action by lining and levelling up the machines, scotching the wheels, tensioning the belts, fitting the correct size sieves for the crop you are about to thresh, adjusting the corn screen, oiling round all the bearings, sweeping the boiler flues, checking that there are no clinkers in the fire-box and making sure that the engine has sufficient head of steam for the task on hand, you may think that you can relax, but you would be well advised not to let down your guard as your troubles may have only just begun.

The chances are that you will have only been running for a few minutes when the farmer complains that the beaters are not knocking out all the corn from the ears and that if you carry on like this you will bankrupt him. At this juncture you point out as tactfully as possible that the sheaves near the top of the rick are wet where the rain has penetrated the thatch and that all will be well as soon as the wet patch is cleared.

"Black Jack" threshing at Little Chalfont Circa 1947. Group from left to right. George Ginger, Frank Pratley, Tom Coote, Dan Williamson, Ted Kaley, unknown man and wife, Bill Blake, Dickie Groom, Bill Darvell, and Harold Hearn on engine.

The farmer invariably remains unconvinced and returns a few minutes later to point out that kernels of grain are blowing out with the chaff. You make a show of adjusting the blowers and reducing the draught only to find that he rebukes you for not blowing the chaff clear from the grain. Furthermore, he snorts, the sample of grain coming out of the corn-shutes into the sack, leaves much to be desired. There is either too much or too little shrivelled or second grade grain entering one sack or another.

If you happen to be threshing barley or bearded wheat he will want to know why some of the awns are still on the grain, and tells you in no uncertain terms that he never experiences all this catalogue of troubles when George Ruff or some other favourite driver of his is in charge.

Whilst all this dialogue is taking place you are, of course, leaving the engine to look after itself, having made sure beforehand that there is plenty of water in the glass and enough coal on the fire to last for a time. Just as you think that you have mollified the customer and things are under control the safety valves on the engine give vent and a shocked look comes over the face of your client as he sees the steam escaping to the atmosphere and he quickly calculates how much of his precious coal you are wasting.

And there was always the dust. Dust clouds in varying volumes, billowed from the threshing machine to offend the nostrils, choke the lungs, parch the throat and play havoc with the eyes and ears.

Clayton & Shuttleworth 40691 heads for farms in the Bovingdon area of Hertfordshire Circa 1930. Driver E Burgin (Ding) . Owner T.T.B.

Dust resulting from many causes including mould and mildew permeated everything. In those days before crop spraying was introduced, noxious weeds abounded on most farms and they were all harvested together with the corn into ricks. By threshing time the sheaves were dry and the dust from the weed seeds formed an amalgam, with other dust, into a witch's brew concocted of ingredients not unlike itching powder. Thistle-down too, frequently blew everywhere and at its worst transformed the entire threshing crew into snow-men and clung to the oily parts of the machinery like limpets. Some crops suffered from a disease called Smut which had the appearance of soot, so when threshing crops suffering from this disease, the threshing crews turned black. In some respects thresher folk were not unlike "Black and White Minstrels"!

The driver, of course, exercised his cunning whenever possible and if he had a choice, set the plant up so that the wind was behind the engine and the dust blew forward away from his work station. Such an arrangement did not suit the unfortunate characters working at the receiving end of the dust but it was not possible to please everyone. It did not help the farmer either as he frequently stationed himself at the corn sacks and with the wind behind the engine he received the full benefit of the smoke and soot being discharged from the funnel of the engine. At the end of the day he resembled a smoked kipper and in a way this was poetic justice as often farmers tried to save money by purchasing cheap coal which gave off excessive quantities of smoke and very little heat, creating problems for the driver as, with such fuel, he experienced difficulty in keeping up the required head of steam.

A very old Fowler threshing at Cherry Tree, Bellingdon in the 1890s. Note unusual pattern of strakes on rear wheels. Driver with oil can Will Hearn (Shute). Owner T.T.B.

The menace from the plague of dust intensified as the season progressed. It was tolerable at harvest time but by the Spring, after rats and mice had occupied the ricks all through the winter and had nibbled the grain, conditions became unpleasant: by May and June they were well-nigh unbearable especially when compounded with hot weather.

In the days before self-feeders, chaff and cavings blowers, and other labour-saving devices became common, a team of up to a dozen people was thought to be necessary for the economic operation of a steam threshing set. Few farmers had so many employees of their own available and relied on casual labour following the set from farm to farm. It was in the driver's interest to encourage as many followers as possible to keep with him, as it was a great convenience to farmers if he arrived with enough labour to allow him to start work without recourse to borrowing help from his neighbours. As the threshing machine owner, driver and others were only paid by the farmer for the hours the set was actually "on the belt", it was important to eliminate as many waiting hours and delays as possible. The driver was also judged on his ability to attract and control the followers which in itself called for the wisdom of Solomon.

65

Davey Paxman baling near Redbourn, Herts 1944. Driver Bill Rust . Owner T.T.B

Of one thing you can be quite sure; when, after a lapse of many months the farmer reluctantly negotiated a settlement of his account with your employer, all your faults would be exaggerated and recounted. Adjustments would have to be made, and a compromise reached, to compensate him for your trespasses and sins of omission or commission.

The trials and troubles of a steam threshing driver were brought home to me quite forcibly and unexpectedly when I was very young and inexperienced. News reached my father one Sunday evening that one of his best drivers, Sammy Fisher, had been killed whilst out for a drive in his car. Sammy's threshing set was at one of our valued but fastidious customers at Castle Hill, Berkhamsted. The farmer naturally expected a driver to report for duty on the Monday morning but at such short notice who was that driver to be? I had a limited amount of threshing experience under supervision but had never taken complete charge of a set. However, someone had to step into the breach and I volunteered.

Very early on the Monday morning, with a sad heart, I made my way to the farm, and lit the fire in the Davey Paxman engine. Sammy's mate duly arrived and we set about preparing for the busy day ahead. To my chagrin I discovered that we were to be engaged with what was known as double work. This involved the use of a chaff-cutter behind the thresher driven from a double pulley on the drum. Although I had seen the job done by others on many occasions, I had never actually operated such a set-up myself.

Ransomes 13696 on double work near Chipperfield Circa 1937. Driver Will Harris . Owner T.T.B.

When engaged on double work the driver has all the problems alluded to earlier plus, of course, any complications created by the Chaff Cutter. The knives on a busy cutter become blunt after two hours of use and have to be sharpened. In order to maintain continuous operations two cutter wheels are provided, each having four, five or six knives according to the make and model. One wheel is in use whilst the other is being sharpened, a chore which the harassed driver has to perform in addition to his other preoccupations. The sharpening process involves the use of files and/or special Carborundum stones because the blades have to be really keen and finely honed. It is an exacting job at the best of times but if you have never done it before, and the farmer is breathing down your neck it is extremely daunting to say the least.

In the event I did my best, but it was not a very satisfactory job and the blades did not cut as well as they should which made the life of the man feeding the machine difficult. Certainly, the episode did nothing to enhance my image or my ego.

Chapter XII

THE ANXIOUS YEARS

Fowler "Russian" type compound 14939 with cultivator at Gt. Green Street Farm, Chenies Circa 1934
Owner T.T.B.

Towards the end of my school days, discussions often took place on the possibility of war and the strategy which should be adopted to combat the threat from Germany about which many were beginning to feel uneasy. Some of the boys thought that a powerful Navy was the answer, others that Air Power was more appropriate. My friend Blackshaw claimed that for the cost of one Battleship, enough aircraft and bombs could be purchased to blow the entire German Navy out of the water. Sadly, as a Flight Lieutenant in R.A.F. he lost his life soon after the outbreak of hostilities whilst putting his theory into practice by attacking enemy shipping in the North Sea.

Few, if any of us, worried very much about the prospects of conflict as we left school and started our experience in the real world of commerce and work. By the middle of the 1930s the depression which followed the first world war was very gradually beginning to lift and hope was returning slowly to the farming community as commodity prices began to edge above the disastrous levels of earlier years. Some of the farms which had been abandoned found tenants and my father was able to find a limited amount of work for his steam ploughing tackle.

If there was one job that I enjoyed more than another it was driving a steam ploughing engine and although it was quite demanding work involving long hours, black hands and an oily face, I liked it and spent many happy weeks high up in the Chilterns working in the fields in all weathers.

Wallis & Steevens Expansion Engine clearing land at Bassingbourne Nr. Royston, Herts for the Airfield made famous by the American Air Force daylight raids on Europe during World War Two. Driver Mark Hobbs, Owner T.T.B.

Several of my friends had chosen more adventurous callings and had joined the R.A.F.. One summer evening as I was "pulling" whilst steam cultivating at Cowcroft Farm above Chesham, I was surprised and pleased to see my close friend from childhood Peter St. John, coming into the field, resplendent in the uniform of a Pilot officer, his recently acquired wings proudly displayed on his chest. I gave him a resounding welcome by blasting on the whistle.

As time went on it became clear that the government was responding to the build-up of arms on the continent, and a number of fighter aerodromes and other installations were commissioned in the Home Counties and elsewhere. Land had to be cleared and trees uprooted to make way for these developments. Many of my father's engines and men were engaged on this work for some years right up to and beyond the outbreak of World War Two.

In due course, the sabre-rattling Mussolini invaded Abyssinia and Hitler was rising to ominous power in Germany. At this juncture I decided to visit the continent to see at first hand what was going on.

My father had provided me with a brand new Morris "Eight" which I used in the business visiting farmers, promoting and marketing our services. He gave me permission to use the car for a trip across Europe.

An unusual type steam roller in South Eastern France.

Together with my good friend Stephen Carruthers we set off for France crossing from Dover to Calais on the Auto-carrier, a small vessel on to which cars had to be hoisted by crane. In those days touring by car on the continent was not the popular pursuit that it is today and there were only half a dozen or so cars on the boat. It is interesting that, a few short years later, the Auto-Carrier played a very different and vital role as it actively assisted with the evacuation of the B.E.F. from Dunkirk in 1940.

In France, the first few hours were spent passing through the battle-field areas of World War One, and although the Armistice had been signed eighteen years earlier the whole scene still bore signs of the conflict and there were few if any mature trees to be seen. We saw many war cemeteries and visited the Canadian Memorial at Vimy Ridge near Arras. The thought that any nations would be mad enough to repeat such diabolical slaughter seemed too remote to contemplate.

As we headed South East I kept a sharp look out for steam engines but apart from trains there were none to be seen. There were plenty of road rollers but they were all powered by internal combustion engines which were of no interest to me. In short I found Northern France to be quite boring. There were a few steam rollers scattered over a wide area down towards Switzerland and I was able to capture some on celluloid during subsequent trips.

It was early in the year and many of the Alpine passes were blocked with snow so we had to plan our route with care. Upon the advice of local Swiss authorities we chose the St. Julier and Maloya passes and, in spite of poor road conditions and not a few hazards, we crossed the Alps safely.

70

The author's Morris "Eight" near the Swiss/Italian border at Chiavenna.

We entered Italy through the border check point at Chiavenna and for the first time we had a taste of the Fascist regime. The British were not popular in Italy at that time as Anthony Eden had been involved with the United Nations in imposing sanctions over the Abyssinian affair and there were placards everywhere showing his portrait on which cancellation marks prominently showed the disapproval of the Fascists.

Consequently, we were kept waiting and our documents were checked and rechecked in a most officious manner whilst other nationals were allowed to pass more freely. Stephen could speak Italian fluently because, as a boy, he had spent many years in Italy where his father had taught English at Milan University. He was able to use his knowledge of the tongue to good advantage and eventually we cleared customs and were on our way along the shores of beautiful lake Como.

Heading South and West for Milan and Turin we travelled on Auto-Stradas for the first time and I was very impressed as Motorways had not at that time been introduced to England and the benefits were obvious. The roads were thronging with little Fiat cars called Topolinos which I was told can be translated in English as Mice. It was interesting to pass the factory in Turin where they were built which had a test track on the roof at that time.

Steam tram in the streets of Novi Ligure, Northern Italy.

After leaving Turin we visited Novi Ligure where I met some of Stephen's friends, enjoyed wonderful hospitality, and was introduced to the Italian sparkling wine Asti Spumenti. The town also had other diversions for me as there was a steam tram plying its trade in the streets. In the countryside I spotted a traction engine on a farm, to say nothing of some attractive young girls among Stephen's friends.

On the coast road near Genoa we came across two steam rollers one of which was of unusual design, probably locally built. Later I was pleased to see a Rochester-made Aveling & Porter at work. We climbed the leaning tower at Pisa and spent two days sight-seeing in Rome, where Mussolini was celebrating his first Empire day. The whole city was bristling with troops parading in lavish uniforms with feathers in their hats. Hundreds of soldiers from the recently overrun Ethiopia were also marching through the streets which were thronging with wildly cheering Italians all making the Fascist salute.

All over Italy pictures of "Il Duce" were prominent on buildings and hoardings and great play was made of his achievements. The railway station at Milan was like a palace and the trains ran on time. The whole populace was under surveillance and if anyone stepped out of line they were subjected to massive doses of Caster Oil.

Fowler "Superba" or Z7 Steam Ploughing engines near Aprillia in the Pontine Marshes, South of Rome.1937.

A project of which Mussolini was particularly boastful and rightly proud was the drainage of the Pontine Marshes south of Rome which he transformed into productive agricultural use, to the great benefit of the entire region. I shared his enthusiasm for this development, not because of its success, although I admired it, but on account of the machinery and plant that he imported to carry out the scheme.

The equipment used included a number of Fowler "Superba" and Z7. compound steam ploughing engines together with a whole range of ploughing, cultivating and drainage implements. These engines were the largest built at the Leeds works and I was thrilled to see a pair of them standing near the side of the road as we approached Aprillia on our way to the beautiful Bay of Naples.

On the way home we crossed the central mountain range to the Adriatic coast and made our way up to Venice. I was most interested to see the sights of this unique city with which I fell in love instantly. At that time some of the water buses were steam driven, a point which was not lost on me. We passed some steam rollers at work between Venice and Verona but could not stop due to heavy traffic congestion which was a pity as they were single crank compounds similar to Burrells and I would have liked some photos of them.

Steam Water bus in the canals of Venice, Italy 1937.

Our little car behaved impeccably and covered the four thousand mile trip admirably. Apart from one puncture and a brake adjustment after crossing the Alpine range we had no trouble whatsoever and arrived in England just in time for Easter. The Kent countryside was a rich lush green of a hue not seen on the continent and as we neared Rochester we passed an Aveling Steam tractor belonging to the Kent County Council quietly simmering by the side of the road after a day's work. It had reversed into a gateway which had a back drop of fine mature trees and formed, to my mind, a beautiful picture. Wisps of steam were being emitted from the cylinder drain cocks and, to me, it was the epitome of permanence, tranquillity and stability.

After the excitement of our adventure, coupled with apprehension about the future of peace in Europe, we felt a warm sense of welcome. It was good to be back.

Chapter XIII

THE CRISIS DEEPENS

Fowler Compound Roller Makers Number 7129, a regular visitor to Northants for the tar spraying contracts. Driver Frank Honey . Owner T.T.B.

The political developments in Europe had little effect on our business except to bring us more trade especially in connection with the clearing of land for aerodromes and government establishments. My father was still active in those pre-war days and my brother and I reported to him. He gave us clearly defined responsibilities and we all worked amicably together. My brother looked after the transport and land clearance whilst I concentrated on agricultural contracting. We had to be flexible because the agricultural work was seasonal and men were transferred from division to division according to the work load. In this way we were kept busy all the year round.

By this time steam rolling was restricted to tar spraying for the most part, and every year seven or eight engines were sent to Northamptonshire to spend the summer on this work. This initiative brought us into contact with Esmond Kimbell who helped us by seconding some of his threshing drivers to us for the season. He has remained a firm friend ever since.

In the agricultural division we still relied heavily on steam and the threshing sets were drawn and driven by traction engines. By 1937 the road transport division started replacing steam with diesel vehicles the first of which was a Foden timber tractor which had the five cylinder Gardner engine fitted crossways behind the cab.

Foden Diesel Timber Tractor with transverse Gardner 5LW engine behind cab, hauling timber from Woburn Park, Beds. Driver Charles Hosier . Owner T.T.B.

An opportunity arose to extend our agricultural business into the Tring area of Hertfordshire when Fred Philby, a threshing contractor of New Mill, died and his widow sold their equipment at auction. My father and I attended the sale, bought some items, and persuaded the principal driver Tom Edwards (Yomi) to join us. Competition was fierce and I had my work cut out to hold the round together but as long as I had Yomi I was in with a chance. After a time things settled down and from the bridgehead at Tring we were able to annex more territory and expand the business. It was a good lesson in diplomacy and I soon learnt to be polite to farmers' wives and daughters.

All the time this exercise was taking place events in Europe were developing fast. The Spanish Civil War was enjoined, an episode in which one of my school friends participated. I cannot remember on which side he fought, but knowing him I would think that it was probably the loser as he always seemed to be unlucky. He lived to tell the tale however. And then Hitler invaded Czechoslovakia and we all thought that the balloon would go up until Neville Chamberlain returned with his piece of paper and we settled down to an uneasy peace for a little longer.

During the early part of 1939 the formation of the Militia was announced. All twenty-year-olds were involved and I, together with all the rest, registered for military service.

Wallis & Steevens Expansion threshing at Stocks Farm, Aldbury near Tring, Herts. Circa 1940 Driver Tom Edwards (Yomi). Owner T.T.B. Photo J. Mullett.

Whilst I was preoccupied with building up the Agricultural division my brother was no less busy doing the same with the timber transport side. We were still running some overtype steam tractors but were introducing diesels all the time. In late 1938 we took on a contract to collect timber from Cornwall and deliver it to Woolwich Arsenal and other locations in the Home Counties. The timber was located in a deep ravine and great skill was needed to extract it from the forest. My brother bought a brand new Caterpiller D4 tractor off the stand at the Smithfield Show for this contract. He also purchased an A.E.C. Diesel articulated timber waggon to do the road work. The trusty Dan Williamson drove the crawler and the intrepid Sydney Brightman handled the truck. Dan's wife Ivy played an important supporting role measuring the trees on the Cornish site, where they occupied a thatched cottage on the estate. Between them all they did a fine job as always.

Nearer home, thousands of beech trees from the Hughendon woods came on to the market and we secured the contract to fell and deliver the whole stand to the sawmills in Princes Risborough at a ridiculously low price forced by intense competition. Due to great ingenuity on the part of my brother, Dickie Groom, the Dunkely Brothers and the dedicated enthusiasm of the workforce, the contract was profitable and vindicated our decision to purchase a new Foden Diesel S.T.G. timber tractor and trailer to add to our growing fleet. Sydney Ratcliffe drove the Foden with distinction, consistent with his record of a lifetime of service to our company.

A.E.C. Diesel loaded with Caterpillar D.4 used to haul timber from Cornwall to London 1938. Driver Sydney Brightman. Owner T.T.B.

Meanwhile ominous war clouds were gathering in Europe and preparations for the defence of our realm were becoming all too evident. Hitler was amassing a gigantic Luftwaffe, so we understood, and he was building pocket battleships and tanks. Everyone here was issued with a gas mask and lists of children's names from the big cities were compiled to assist with evacuation. Rumours spread that thousands of coffins were being stored in London to take care of casualties from expected air-raids, and every weekend the skies buzzed with light aircraft as volunteer reserve pilots learnt to fly.

My friend Peter was at Debden in Essex flying Hurricanes and I was awaiting my call-up papers. It seemed a very good time to take a holiday together whilst we had the chance. I had by then acquired a Wolseley Hornet Eustace Watkins Special sports car, in which we set off for the West Country. Crossing Salisbury Plain we could not help noticing the activity on the military camps where wooden huts were springing up like mushrooms and it was clear that something big was in the wind.

We spent the night in Torquay with friends and visited our timber extraction operations in Cornwall before heading for Lands End. We saw some of Dingle's fine fleet of modern steam rollers at work on the roads, and in the Barnstaple area came across a lovely Burrell compound road engine hauling timber. It was a super trip which we both thoroughly enjoyed.

The author with his friend P.C.B. St. John at Clovelly June 1939.

After our holiday, which was in June 1939, our lives settled back into a normal pattern. Peter returned to his squadron and I set about getting the equipment ready for the coming harvest. Straw was beginning to find a market when baled, so my brother and I visited the Royal Show and bought a new Davis baler to work behind our threshing sets. It was fitted with a self-feeder and proved to be a very fine and reliable machine, putting us well ahead of any competition in our area.

In July the first draft of Militia was called up and some of my friends were among those that reported to a camp in Oswestry. August came and still I heard nothing from the military authorities but tension was rising in Europe and it became increasingly clear that the Nazis were bent on trouble. Events took a nasty turn when they made a pact with Russia.

At home visitors called as usual and among them my father's friend Major Ind, from Dedham Hall in Suffolk, dropped in from time to time to take tea or sally forth into the countryside in search of rare or historic engines, which he could photograph to add to his splendid collection.

Right on cue the corn ripened and harvest was upon us as usual, Hitler or no Hitler, and the threshing sets steamed off to the fields and farms to carry out their essential tasks. During the last week of August my orders came through. I was to report to the R.A.O.C. Hillsea Barracks at Portsmouth on the 15th September, in just three weeks' time. A single one-way ticket was enclosed.

Harry Shepherd (on left of picture) takes an interest in Davey Paxman engine. Owner T.T.B.

Maclaren baling near St. Albans during the war. Driver Frank Pratley. Owner T.T.B.

At about this time our old friend Harry Shepherd arrived and presented us with a bag containing one hundred weight of sugar and a large bunch of bananas. He explained that he did not like the look of the international situation and thought that the sugar might come in handy. His comment turned out to be the understatement of the year.

A week later the Germans marched into Poland, Peter's squadron was ordered to fly to Northern France and we were at war.

Chapter XIV

THE WAR MACHINE

Fatal accident at Bell Lane, near Latimer, involving Foden "D" type steam tractor belonging to Francis Grover (In road on left of picture talking to T.T.B.) Driver George Harris lost his life.

Needless to say, the declaration of war was only the beginning of a series of actions necessary to put the nation and the Commonwealth on to a war footing. The reservists and Territorial Battalions were called up immediately and the manpower requirements were reviewed. The Militia, in which I was involved, were also called to the colours regardless of their occupation.

New government departments were formed and priorities were given to those activities deemed to be essential to the war effort. The two main divisions of our business reported to their own govenment department. The transport side, run by my brother, came under the control of the "Home Grown Timber Department" of the Board of Trade and the agricultural division which I had been running, until I was called up, took its orders from The Country Agricultural Committees covering the areas in which we operated. Our plant hire, involving our steam rollers, did not report to any one in particular.

The change over to gearing up for war took some time and the exercise was not resolved overnight. It was clear that the divisions of our company would have to be dramatically expanded to meet the demands to be made upon them and my brother made a start by purchasing an extra new Foden Diesel Timber Tractor and a new Caterpillar to extract timber from the forests.

Moving a large boiler for Mr. George Evans of Wiggington (fourth from right of picture).
Driver Sydney Ratcliffe.

The processes of agriculture are of course governed by well-defined natural laws involving life cycles which cannot be hurried, regardless of the exigencies of war or anything else; so the size of the 1939 harvest was determined long before the war started and it could not be altered. The threat from submarine warfare called for increased acreages of cereal crops, and the vast areas of land that had been laid down to grass between the wars had to be ploughed and sown as quickly as practicable. By this means the amount of land under cereals in 1940 was probably double that of the previous year.

In turn the crops had to be harvested, built into ricks or stored in barns and eventually threshed. All this work had to be undertaken by an industry which had been run down in peace time and where a shortage of skilled and experienced operators existed on the scale required.

The Women's Land Army was formed and pensioners were encouraged to return to the industry to help as much as possible and to train newcomers in the arts of rick building, thatching and other essentials. The Combine Harvester had not at that time penetrated the British market on any scale and its potential was not realised, with the result that the methods used in agriculture were little different from those that had been practised for the previous seventy years or so. Much of the threshing was still carried out by steam and it was labour intensive.

Wartime threshing scene at Potten End, Nr. Berkhamsted, Herts. Italian prisoners of war can be seen on the rick and by the corn sacks. Driver A Philbey M.M. and bar. Engine Fowler 11698 . Owner T.T.B.

The threshing of the 1939 harvest created no particular problems, but it was clear that the following and subsequent harvests would be a very different matter, and the prospect caused some concern to the agricultural community and those responsible for it.

In spite of advancing years and indifferent health my ageing father took over my duties when I was called up and kept things together during that first winter of the war, with help from my brother who had enough on his hands already dealing with the timber and transport division. When asked by the authorities if he could double or treble his capacity for threshing for the duration of the war, my father had to admit that, with all the will in the world, at his age, he could not do so.

He was asked if he could meet the requirements if I was released from the Army. He offered to hear what I had to say and accordingly wrote to me to get my reaction to the idea.

Meanwhile, I was undergoing initial training and becoming proficient at marching, saluting, peeling potatoes, digging slit trenches, cleaning latrines, polishing boots and all the other things that recruits are expected to do. The army was suffering from a massive dose of indigestion as thousands of men were called up before they could be absorbed and the whole atmosphere was one of organised chaos.

83

Little Chalfront Home Guard Infantry platoon. Author in middle of centre row.

It seemed to me that, until the army got its act together, the whole exercise was a waste of time so when my father wrote to ask if I would be willing to return to the business if asked to do so, I agreed and accepted the suggestion with some fortitude. The mills of authority grind exceedingly slowly especially in war time, and it was some months before I heard any more.

In due course, I passed out of the R.A.O.C. training establishment, my experience in the business at home having stood me in good stead as I completed the trade tests without difficulty. As a qualified R.A.O.C. technician I was attached to the 4th Battalion Cheshire Regiment, and served in the Motor Transport Company. The regiment was stationed in the village of Letcombe Regis in the Berkshire Downs, near Wantage, and was about to join the B.E.F. in France. The Ox & Bucks, with whom the Cheshires were to join forces later in France were, like us, roughing it, and were stationed on the side of the Bath Road at Marlborough.

Having heard no more of the plan to return home I settled down to the life of a war-time soldier and adjusted to the rough and tumble of active service as thousands of others were doing at that time. Eventually, when I had almost given up the thought of returning to the business I was called before the Commanding Officer, and ordered to pack my bags and return to Amersham. I was enrolled on to the Army Reserve which meant that I could be recalled at a moment's notice, and was instructed to keep my uniform which came in useful when I served in the Home Guard which was formed at about that time. I could not help being slightly put out by the relaxed way that the War Office seemed able to manage without me!

Chapter XV

A CLOSE CALL

Clayton & Shuttleworth engine similar to the one purchased from Coln Rogers, Gloucestershire
Photo shows engine when in the ownership of the author.

Back at the ranch, as they say, the threshing season was drawing to a close when I returned; consequently, I was able to address the problem of preparing for the 1940 bumper cereal harvest with a single mind. None of the other threshing contractors in the area were planning to increase their capacity so it was clear that our number of sets should be increased from four to eight. Furthermore, as we had sold our steam ploughing engines when they were no longer needed before the war, it was desirable to acquire and commission another set.

During my spell with the Cheshires I had kept my ear to the ground, and from enquiries that I had made, had reason to believe that some threshing tackle was standing idle in the stinging nettles in the vacinity of Bibury, Gloucestershire. As we needed more plant to fulfil our requirements, I made my way to the location and sure enough the information was correct and I was able to buy three very fine engines and a threshing drum from Mrs. Guest the widow of the late Albert Guest, a well known and respected engine owner whose business was operated from Coln Rogers in the Costwolds. The engines comprised a fine upstanding Clayton & Shuttleworth, a Wallis & Steevens Compound, and an Allchin. The drum was a Ruston. I also bought a Ransomes Sims and Jefferies engine, which had seen little service, from a farmer at Bibury.

Wallis & Steevens Compound purchased from Mrs. Guest, Coln Rogers. Photo shows engine approaching Chartridge, near Chesham. Driver Stanley Sear. Owner T.T.B. Photo J Mullett.

It is a great tribute to the owners and drivers of the engines that in spite of standing unused in the open for some years, all the engines were in working order and steamable. They had been well looked after and carefully wrapped up and well oiled when they were laid up.

In due course, taking three trusted and experienced men with me, I travelled to Gloucestershire to steam the engines home to Amersham. Leaving Stanley Blunt and one other helper at Bibury to raise steam in the Ransomes, George Hearn and I proceeded to Coln Rogers where we steamed the Clayton. We had taken "A" shaped draw bars with us and we used these to couple the other two engines behind us.

It was a beautiful summer evening as I proudly drove our little convoy out of the farmyard and headed into the village, where it seemed that the entire population had turned out to pay tribute and say farewell to the engines that for so long had been a feature of local community life.

I had never driven traction engines in the Cotswolds before and did not realise how steep the hills were. I was soon to learn the hard way as other engine drivers had done before me.

Allchin engine, one of the cavalcade involved in the accident at Bibury. Photo depicts engine at Haresfoot Farm, Berkhamsted. Driver George Burgin. Owner T.T.B. Photo J Mullett.

Almost as soon as we had started our journey the gauge or sight glass shattered and I had to hastily shut the cocks, albeit with some difficulty. From then on I had to speculate on how much water there was in the boiler as I had no visual aid, a problem with which all drivers are familiar from time to time. I could not turn back so I decided to press on; after all our immediate objective was to spend the night at Bibury which was only a few miles distant. As we started to climb the sharp hill by the church in Coln Rogers the wheels on the Clayton spun and we came to a halt. The load behind was too much and we had to uncouple one of the trailing engines and take them up one at a time. The penny did not drop that other equally steep hills might lie ahead!

At last we waved farewell to the villagers and steamed on our way. After a time the vibration of the steel wheels disturbed the sediment in the boiler water feed pipes and some grit became lodged under the valve in the boiler clack box causing steam to blow back into the water tank heating up the feed water. This in turn prevented the boiler feed injector from working as such devices do not like warm water.

By this time I was getting anxious as with no sight glass, no injector, a temperamental boiler feed pump, a strange road and fading light, my problems were multiplying. With less than half a mile to go the safety of friends in Bibury however, I was not too worried.

Ransomes Sims & Jeffery engine purchased from Bibury. Photo shows engine threshing near Redbourne, Herts. Driver Bill Rust . Owner T.T.B.

I changed into a low gear to descend the hill into the village and slowly edged over the brow. Holding the engine back on the reverse all went well until the combined weight of the three engines coupled together exceeded the ability of the steel driving wheels on the Clayton to grip on the granite chippings on the road surface.

It is impossible to describe the next few minutes which were possibly the most hair-raising of my life. The cavalcade rapidly gathered speed and became completely uncontrollable, not unlike a mighty avalanche. To jump could have invited instant death. Our only chance was to stay on the footplate in the hope that the engine would not overturn. George Hearn (Nipper) did a fantastic job on the steering, drawing on his immense skill and experience. He kept us straight for a time but in the end the whole outfit-jack knifed. One hind wheel on the Clayton rose from the ground and the engine hung precariously in the balance before crashing back onto all fours, completely blocking the road. It was an almighty pile up from which George and I miracously escaped unscathed and no lasting damage was done to the engines either. It was a close call.

It was well after midnight before we were able to get the engines off the road and under the watchful eye of the local policeman get some semblance of order out of the chaos. Without further mishap the engines reached Amersham safely in due course.

"Black Jack" driving thresher restored after spending many years derelict in the stinging nettles. Driver Dave Sear. Owner T.T.B.

In addition to the above we were able to acquire a little-used Fowler threshing engine 10388 from the Pendley Stock Farms, Tring. We were to require much more plant later.

It now remained for us to get enough threshing machines, trussers, balers, and chaff-cutters to match the engines. This part of the programme was not too formidable as there were quite a few of these items which had fallen into disuse during the farming depression of the 1920's, standing derelict in the countryside. Of course, they were in a pitiful state and had to be rebuilt, but we had a fine team of experienced and dedicated people able and willing to carry out the work involved. My father knew most of the owners well so we had no difficulty in buying the equipment to complete our plans.

Our search for equipment took us to many parts of the country. We visited a number of auction sales, one of which was at Baldock, Herts where the Deans were selling their threshing and steam ploughing tackle. The sale was well attended and we met a number of old friends including Frank Wilder of Crowmarsh and John Turney, the well known steam ploughing and dredging contractor from Weston-on-the-Green, who bought a threshing machine and Fowler cultivator respectively. My father bought an Innes Chaff-cutter and offered to collect the thresher and cultivator for his friends. The following week I set off early one morning driving our Foden "D" type "King of the Forest" steam timber tractor to tow the purchases back to Amersham. The journey involved travelling forty miles each way and as the thresher was on wooden wheels I dared not travel at much more than walking speed on the way back for fear of shaking it to pieces. Jack Pearce stoked for me and we were both quite weary by the time we reached our base just before dark.

Chapter XVI

STEAM PLOUGHING IN WARTIME

Fowler 14252 "King George" cultivating near Chalfont St. Giles during World War 2.
Driver Frank Honey Owner T.T.B. Photo J Mullett.

During a conversation at the Baldock sale John Turney mentioned to my father that he had a pair of Fowler Compound steam ploughing engines surplus to his requirements and offered them to us.

At that stage in the war thousands of acres of grass land were scheduled to be ploughed up and large areas had to be drained as well. As we were well known for steam ploughing and cultivating from the early nineteen hundreds onwards many farmers asked us if we could re-enter the steam ploughing scene.

The war Agricultural Committees were also in favour of the idea so my father decided to visit Weston-on-the-Green and have a look at the engines. It has been said that my father had a long standing love affair with engines of all sorts and that he was emotionally involved with them, especially Fowlers. Be that as it may, he could not resist the temptation of acquiring King Albert & King George numbered 14351 and 14352.

It was a great moment for me when, watched by my father, I steamed King Albert out of the shed where it had been stored. As my father said at the time "it handled like a kitten". King George needed a little attention so it was towed back to Amersham behind its workmate, with Frank Honey driving.

Fowler compound "King Albert" cultivating near Chenies, Bucks. Circa 1942.
Driver Will Hearn (Shute). Owner T.T.B.

Within a fortnight of getting the engines home, they were out at work cultivating in the village of Wilstone near Tring. They were in great demand and it was difficult to know which job to do first.

As the war effort developed, a large acreage of wet land in the Long Marston area of Hertfordshire was earmarked to be ploughed but it had to be mole drained first. We were offered the job and decided to take on the work. There were, however, two snags; we had no mole drainer and the winding drums on our engines only held six hundred yards of rope whereas the job called for eight hundred yards.

The first problem was solved by a visit to Walter Keeling, Crays Hill, Billericay, who had advertised a Fowler mole drainer for sale. It was in good condition and we were able to buy it from Walter with whom a fine friendship developed. We also bought a Clayton & Shuttleworth threshing machine from him and he put both items on the rail for us. The second problem was overcome by an offer of help from Mr. Briggs, a steam ploughing contractor of Stamford who sold us a pair of drums designed to hold eight hundred yards of rope. Although they had been removed from a pair of Fowler AA engines they fitted King Albert and King George perfectly.

Breaking Clover Ley near Latimer, Bucks. during World War 2 for Bill Simpson, Manor Farm, Chenies. Driver on "King Albert" Bill Darvell, Will Hearn on cultivator and author at rear of engine. Owner T.T.B. Photo Author's collection.

When we visited Walter he was threshing with his fine Burrell and we were impressed by the speed at which the work was being carried out. We soon learnt that threshing contractors in that part of the country threshed by piece work, or by the quarter, hence the urgency. For many months our engines worked away draining hundreds of acres of low lying land and making it fit for cropping. Coal was in short supply so that drivers had to manage with brickettes which were really compressed coal dust bonded together in some way. I remember poor old Will Hearn (Shute), who must have been seventy years old at the time, rubbing his forehead and weeping with pain as the coal dust made his eyes smart in the hot weather. In spite of this hardship he kept at the controls and never gave up. He was a brave man.

Whether or not an enemy aircraft spotted the smoke from the engines we shall never know but one lunch time the Germans dropped a land mine on the school at Long Marston, near where the engines were working, killing the school mistress. Fortunately, the children had all gone home to dinner so they mercifully escaped.

The engines were mostly used on heavy land, known in the country as "Four horse land" and we used a special four furrow Fowler anti-balance plough with sub-soiler blades for some of this work. It was as much as the engines could do to haul this plough although they handled a six furrow general purpose plough with ease.

92

Fowler BB1 cultivating at Little Chalfont. Driver Harold Hearn. John Bush on cultivator Owner T.T.B.

When steam cultivating, the land was covered twice and sometimes three times over, the second and third at right angles to the previous one. The work became easier after the first time over and the engines could run faster. Pulling the second and third time over the motions and crankshafts on the engines were a blur as the drivers raced them to earn extra bonus or "acre money" as it was known. The engines were beautifully balanced and were designed to run at high speeds when necessary.

During the season especially after harvest, the crews on steam ploughs often worked long hours and one of our foremen, Ernie Haggar, often recalled how he heard the bells of Stevenage Church chime twelve midnight as he was banking down the fire on his engine after a long day.

After the war we sold "King Albert" and "King George" but later bought several sets of Fowler BB1 engines which we ran, as a hobby, on land which we farmed at Little Chalfont near Chenies. We still own a set of engines complete with all the implements and in spite of advancing years hope to have one more go before anno domini finally has the last say, the Great Reaper calls a halt and the whistle finally signals "end of play".

Chapter XVII

THE LULL BEFORE THE STORM.

The Author's father T.T.B. on left of picture. This photo was taken on a visit to Mr. George Cushing, Thursford, Norfolk before his famous museum was opened officially.

There was an impasse in Europe at that time, with the Germans keeping behind the Siegfried Line of fortifications and the Allies doing the same behind the Maginot Line, and this phase of the war became known as the "phoney war". It was a time of tension and speculation, and a popular song in those days among the troops was "Mother, we'll hang your washing on the Siegfried Line, if the Siegfried line's still there".

Early in May, I was working inside a very dusty threshing machine helping to get it ready for harvest, when someone who had been listening to a portable radio, excitedly broke the news to me that the Germans had mounted a massive offensive. It soon transpired that they were invading Luxembourg, Holland and Belgium, circumventing the Maginot Line. The B.E.F. together with some French Divisions moved north to assist the Belgians. My thoughts turned to my friends in the Cheshires and supporting attachments with whom I had been serving so recently, as they faced the onslaught.

The campaign is now, of course, a matter of history, but in those fateful days events were very poignant as the "Blitzkrieg" developed. Supported by paratroopers, dive bombers, squadrons of tanks and armoured columns, the fanatical Huns advanced at an unbelievable speed and in approximately two weeks reached the English Channel, cutting off the B.E.F. from their French Allies to the South. It was a time of great crisis, as over a quarter of a million British troops were in grave danger of being killed or taken prisoner.

Aveling and Porter (Croydon) one of the engines used to clear the land for the anti-tank ditch constructed near Arundel, Sussex during 1940. Owner T.T.B. Photo shows the engine hauling a unique scarifier, ripping up the High Street, at Watford when the surface was re-made in the 1920s.

Winston Churchill became Prime Minister and rallied the nation with some rousing rhetoric, and a national day of prayer was held, in which all of us with friends and relatives in the B.E.F. joined fervently. The nation held its breath whilst the evacuation via Dunkirk was organised and news of our comrades, friends and loved ones was anxiously awaited. Towards the end of the month I received a letter from Jock Romanis, a good friend of mine in the R.O.A.C. attachment, to say that he was safely back in England after spending two horrendous days on the beaches at Dunkirk with forty or so Cheshires. He went on to say that the Cheshires had lost four hundred men and all their equipment.

Years after the war was over Bernard Hardacre who served with the Oxon & Bucks told me that in May 1940 the Cheshires, which was a machine gun regiment, joined with his infantry regiment and held up the German advance near Hazebrouck for three or four days before they were overrun by enemy tanks and taken prisoner.

They were crowded into railway waggons and endured great hardships, privations and malnutrition as they were transported to Poland and suffered five and a half years as Prisoners of War.

At one point as their train pulled into a deserted railay station a lone German called out to Bernard; "Tommy, who is going to hang your mother's washing on the Siegfried Line now?".

Ransome Sims & Jefferies engine 13696 used on land clearance for the anti-tank ditch in Sussex. Driver Frank Beaumont (Jasper) Photo shows the engine being driven by Frank Honey. Owner T.T.B.

The R.A.F. pulled back the fighter squadrons to England and my friend Peter was transferred to 74 Squadron, flying Spitfires under the command of the famous ace "Sailor" Malan.

It became clear that Hitler meant to invade England if he could and defences were strengthened accordingly. The main deterrent was the R.A.F., but in addition the Home Guard was formed and an anti-tank ditch was constructed along the South coast. Land had to be cleared to make way for the ditch, so three of our traction engines were engaged on this work. The urgency of the work required continuous operation week day and Sunday which did not please the wives of the drivers as their men were away for weeks on end. Fortunately all the difficulties were overcome and the ditch was completed quickly and, as it turned out, was never needed as the R.A.F. kept the Nazis at bay.

In the meantime, I was preoccupied with preparations for harvest, and a team of enthusiasts under the leadership of George Ruff was working flat out restoring derelict threshing tackle as the factories making new agricultural machines could not deliver fast enought to meet the tremendous demand.

One day, as Alf Scot (Scottie) our chief carpenter, a highly valued member of the team was working on top of a threshing drum, a Spitfire swooped out of the sun and skimmed over his head before soaring off in the general direction of Northolt. Of course, we all know who the pilot was but no one let on, as low flying was frowned on officially and nobody wanted to see Peter get into trouble. It was common knowledge at the time that Scottie had to return home for a clean set of underwear as a result of this incident.

Chapter XVIII

ALL STATIONS GO

George Ruff driving "Black Jack" near Chenies before the war. Note the spare knife wheel from the Maynard Chaff Cutter the blades of which had to be kept razor sharp. Owner T.T.B.

Getting the equipment ready for the "off" was rather like the tip of an iceberg. There was far more to be done than met the eye. Machinery is one thing, manning is another, especially in wartime.

Before the war and during the first winter George Ruff drove Set No. 1 normally powered by "Black Jack" but with the increased number of sets it was clear that he was needed at our base to take care of the repair, maintenance and rebuilding of equipment and that he could no longer be tied down to the operational aspects of the work. We were, until that time, operating a number of steam rollers and some of the drivers had threshing experience. An opportunity arose to hire out some of the rollers to contractors working for the Royal Navy at Scapa Flow where our drivers were not required. It seemed sensible to send the rollers north for the duration and to use the drivers on priority food and timber production at home.

The transition took some time to organise as contracts had to be completed before drivers could be transferred, so in the absence of anyone else, I took over from George and drove "Black Jack" during the first few weeks of the season.

The Author (on extreme right of picture) driving Fowler 10388 at Bragman's Farm, Sarratt 1940. Owner T.T.B.

It was hot, dry weather and we were able to thresh direct from the stook throughout the month of August threshing from 7.30 a.m. until 9 o'clock at night which proved to be a demanding and tiring programme.

My feeder, or second man, was Jim Hearn, nicknamed "Flute", one of three Hearn brothers, all of whom were well known colourful local characters who rendered a lifetime of sterling service to my father. The other two were Will and George nicknamed Shute and Nipper.

Our first customer was Bill Simpson who had taken over the tenancy of the Manor Farm, Chenies from my uncle Harry. He was a fine farmer and a fair, if hard taskmaster with a great sense of humour. The threshing team was made up of local volunteers including some boys on holiday from school among whom were Trevor Haimes and John Vivian whose paths continued to cross with mine in business friendship for the next half century. Bill kept us all on our toes as we worked from morning to night in the blazing hot sun, and we all remember him with affection.

Upon arriving home after dark during September I met my brother outside our home and he pointed my attention to the direction of London where the sky was lit up so brightly that you could have read a newspaper where we were. The Luftwaffe had bombed the docks and set them on fire. The war was literally hotting up and looking ugly.

Eventually I handed over the threshing set to Dave Sear an experienced veteran driver who had driven Fowler Road Locos in South Africa during the Boer War. By this time George Ruff had prepared another set for action, and as no other drivers had become available, I commissioned it, and drove it myself for some time, until Bill Hearn (Shute) became free when I handed it over to him. The engine was Fowler 10388, new to Rothschilds and similar to "Black Jack". My mate was Jack Scobie, a quiet alert survivor from the infantry in World War One. His years in the trenches had left him with a slight stoop and quick involuntary reactions. He was a good man to have around and was a great help to me. The following season he took on a set himself and did a fine job.

Flying Officer Peter Cape Beauchamp St. John, 74 Squadron R.A.F. killed in action over the Downs near Gatwick whilst flying a Spitfire on the 22nd October 1940. His guns were empty. He had fought to the last round of ammunition.

We threshed in the hills around Sarratt and later in the lovely valley by the River Chess. It was a mellow autumn and a great season for mushrooms which we gathered in abundance. London was being bombed heavily and some girl friends of my sister's took shelter in our home out of the Blitz. My friend Peter was convalescing at Halton Camp Hospital having been wounded in aerial combat defending London and he joined us all for a memorable supper, where mother had prepared the most enormous and delicious platter of field mushrooms imaginable. It was the last meal that we were to have together, as he returned to his squadron at Biggin Hill shortly afterwards, and was shot down and killed in an air battle near Gatwick on the 22nd October. His death was a great blow to me.

Chapter XIX

THE RIFLE BUTT CONTRACT

Fowler 4001 brought out of retirement to load the logs from the Latimer Woodlands. Driver at that time, sixteen year old Oliver Pearce. Owner T.T.B. Photo shows engine when in the ownership of Neddy Gomm who is pictured at the controls.

After the evacuation of Dunkirk the army was short of equipment of all kinds as masses of stores, weapons, workshops and vehicles had to be abandoned and left behind on the continent. The importation of food and raw materials was seriously disrupted by the "U" boat packs so the best possible use had to be made of home grown supplies.

It must have been early in 1941 that we had a visit from a representative of the war cabinet informing us that the entire beech woods on the Latimer Estate were to be cut down. Furthermore, we, (Boughtons) were to handle the extraction and transport of the trees to sawmills at Penn Street and High Wycombe which were being commandeered to convert the timber into munitions. This work was to receive utmost priority regardless of other commitments. It was an order, and we had no option but to comply. A daily quota was to be laid down and closely monitored.

Quite apart from this requirement, timber was in great demand and all services were stretched to the limit. In his efforts to satisfy the needs of our regular timber customers, my brother was as harassed as I was, as I tried to meet the farmers' threshing needs, and the order from Whitehall created quite a problem. No new equipment could be obtained for love or money at that stage in the war, so it was clear that improvisation would have to be the order of the day.

Two Foden Steam Timber Tractors and the Tasker Chain drive "Little Giant" which hauled the trees from the Latimer Estate for the Rifle Butt contract. Owner T.T.B.

It is surprising how local knowledge can help in a situation like the one which faced us. How we came to hear of it I cannot remember but we were able to buy a Caterpillar D6 from a farmer in Weston, Hertfordshire. It was ideal for the extraction of the giant beech trees from the Latimer forests. In the course of our travels in the West Country we had spotted a Tasker "Little Giant" chain drive steam tractor abandoned in a woodland near Newton Abbot and in our hour of need we were able to locate the owner, purchase the little engine, and have it sent by rail to Amersham. The short haul from Latimer to Penn Street was well within its economic range. It needed new tyres and boiler tubes but we restored it quite quickly.

Next we required some trailers for it to haul and by an extraordinary piece of good fortune, we were offered some large six wheeled Chenard Walker trailers, which were surplus to the requirements of George Cohen of London. The purchase and adaptation of the trailers for timber haulage created no problems for us and the Jigsaw was nearly in place.

To complete the picture we only required a winching tractor or engine to parbuckle the trees on to the trailers to save taking the time of the Caterpillar or "Little Giant". The answer to this requirement was soon found. Our good friend Neddy Gomm of Chesham had an old Fowler engine No. 4001 built in 1882 which he had replaced by a more modern Fowler some years earlier. For some reason, sentimental or otherwise, he had not scrapped it. It was still in good working order and he was willing to sell it to us.

Dancer & Hearn's Sawmills, Penn Street where the trees from Latimer were converted into munitions. Later in the war the same factory was used to make wings for Mosquito aircraft.

By the time the formalities for the purchase of the trees from Lord Chesham by the ministry were completed and the tree fellers moved in, we were ready to go. The plan worked like a charm.

The trees were skidded to loading points by the Caterpillar D6 driven by Sam Williamson, where they were rolled on to trailers by the old Fowler driven by the sixteen year old Oliver Pearce. His father Jack Pearce driving the "Little Giant", shuttled the loaded trailers to the sawmills, completing three round trips per day. The task was made possible by the fact that there was always a loaded trailer waiting on its return to the forest. The quota to Penn Street was one thousand cubic feet per day which the team exceeded without difficulty. In addition a quota to the High Wycombe sawmills was taken care of by our Foden steam tractors, leaving the fleet of diesels to carry on with long distance operations undisturbed. Whitehall was satisfied and our regular customers were looked after as well. It was a smooth operation utilising equipment which, for the most part, would have been scrapped but for the war.

Ironically, we had played an active part in the destruction of the beautiful woodlands which we loved so much but "needs must when the Devil drives".

Chapter XX

THE PRESSURES INCREASE

Women's Land Army Girls in action. Photo courtesy of the Times Newspaper.

The arrival of the 1942 harvest caused the demand for threshing capacity to become insatiable, and the pressures on the contractors were enormous. The telephone never stopped ringing and even the weather conspired against us. It seemed to me that it never stopped raining or blowing a gale, both of which conditions prevented the sets from operating, and caused the queues of farmers waiting for the machines to lengthen alarmingly.

To make matters more complicated the ministry brought in an order that, during the early part of the season, no set could thresh more than two ricks on any one farm before moving on to the next. The idea was understandable as the object was go give every farmer a turn, but in practice it was a time-wasting exercise, as the sets spent nearly as much time moving as they did threshing and the overall result was counter-productive. Furthermore an order was made that wire netting had to be placed round the ricks before threshing commenced, to prevent rats and mice escaping. The order was enforced whether there was any vermin in the ricks or not, which made rather a nonsense of the concept at times.

The threshing teams were made up mostly of Women's Land Army girls, many of whom were new to the countryside and it was a toss-up which squealed the loudest, the girls or the rats as the latter were brutally despatched with sticks and pitch forks by all and sundry. Sometimes the mice would find their way into the girls' clothing and there would be a tremendous commotion until things were sorted out.

Women's Land Army Girl Ruby Parsons (nee Harwood) cultivating for the war effort.
Photo courtesy Mrs. Parsons.

My sister Joan was given the job of looking after three hundred Land girls in the county of Bucks by the Ministry. Many of the girls were engaged on threshing and her experiences in dealing with their emotional and other problems would fill volumes if she ever attempted to record them.

By the fourth harvest of the war we had built up our complement of sets to fifteen, all steam driven, and these operated in an area stretching from Aylesbury to Barnet in catering for the needs of some four hundred large and small farmers. In addition we ran a set of steam ploughing engines, fitted with 800 yard rope drums, enabling them to mole drain as well as plough and cultivate. All the sets were extremely busy and the work ceased to be seasonal, so that when hay baling was taken into consideration many of the outfits worked throughout the year with hardly a break for maintenance.

The manning of the sets was a nightmare as there were not enough experienced operatives to go round, and we had to emabark on an intensive training programme. During the years of depression between the wars quite a few drivers had left the industry and had taken up other work. Some had opened shops, others had become gardeners, and many of them were engaged on work which was not essential to the war effort. Quite a number agreed to return to threshing and ploughing for the duration and they made a fine contribution to food production.

Chapter XXI

TIMES OF CRISIS AND CHANGE

Fowler Compound threshing at Ridge Hill, Shenley, Herts 1943. Driver Bill Shepherd Owner T.T.B.

Early in 1943 the threshing officer for Hertfordshire, Sandy Murdoch, came to see us and brought the news that contractors to the north of us had decided to discontinue their threshing business. They were operating thirty steam-driven sets and their territory bordered ours. For years we had been poaching each others' customers when opportunities arose. It was clear that the sets must be kept at work at all costs, and the question was whether we would take over those which operated in Hertfordshire. In any event the Ministry had decided to commandeer the sets at an agreed price and offered to lease them to us for the duration, if we would operate them.

The crisis created a challenge which was hard to resist and after consulting with my father I decided to give it a try and agreed to take over nine threshing sets and two clover hulling outfits provided the crews stayed with them. I duly visited each driver and without exception they joined our company and integrated well. In fact some turned out to be among the finest and most loyal employees that have crossed my path, and although most if not all, have received the home call, having departed this life, I still remember them and the momentous times when we first met.

Our territory was greatly enlarged with the additional plant, and we now covered an area of at least a thousand square miles stretching beyond Baldock on the Great North Road, taking in some excellent arable country.

Fowler Compound threshing at Wood End N.E. Herts 1943. Driver Frank Monk Owner T.T.B.

The annexation of the extra business was not accomplished without problems which soon became apparent. Our own fifteen sets had been modernised and most if not all were equipped with ball bearings, self feeders, chaff and cavings blowers, balers with self-feeders and other improvements, which reduced the number of crew required by at least four. The leased sets had none of these refinements and they had only two balers without self-feeders between them, so that a man had to stand on them and pitchfork the straw into the hoppers.

Baled straw was in demand and the farmers clamoured for a baler with each set, but the snag was that the makers could not produce them fast enough and new ones could not be obtained. To overcome this difficulty we decided to build a batch of balers in our Amersham plant and proceeded to do so.

No sooner had we equipped ourselves with the necessary balers than baling wire was rationed and we were back to square one. Upon enquiry we discovered that the reason for the rationing was not the shortage of wire but the lack of capacity to cut and loop it in the traditional manner. We could in fact obtain all the wire we needed in coils without difficulty. We accordingly set up machinery for cutting and looping which was operated by Frank Cox, disabled from birth, who came to work in a wheel chair. Not only were we able to produce enough baling wire for our own sets but kept other contractors supplied as well, including our friends Walter Keeling of Billericay in Essex, Neddy Gomm of Chesham and others.

Fowler "Nelson" threshing at Bennington, Herts 1943. Driver George Haggar Owner T.T.B.

Catering for the threshing needs of nearly one thousand farmers was no small exercise, as we were dealing with a large cross-section of the agricultural community ranging from the landed gentry with large estates to small-holders with only one rick. Threshing for professional farmers was straightforward enough as years of a "Diamond cut Diamond" relationship had taught us to respect each other, and many of our customers became good friends of mine. The hard cases were the individuals who had been forced to plough up a paddock for the war effort and who did not have a clue about building, thatching, or siting ricks, letting the rain soak into them until they were little better than a soggy mess which blocked the sieves and choked the machines. Often they built the ricks in inaccessible spots and swampy places where our heavy machinery became bogged down and we were presented with well nigh impossible situations.

By the 1944 harvest a dramatic change in the agricultural scene had taken place. The War Agricultural Committees backed and financed by unlimited budgets had indulged in an extravagant orgy of expenditure creating a massive overkill situation. For the first three or four years of the war the industry had been starved of machinery; now it was choked, and unable to digest the huge quantities of new threshers and balers which the Ministry had ordered from factories in England and Scotland. Fosters, Marshalls, Ransomes, Fisher Humphries, Garvies, Denings, Davises, Jones, Powells and others were all pouring machines into the County depots.

Marshall Model "M" threshing near Chalfont St Giles, Bucks. 1945. Driver George Adams Owner T.T.B.

Large new International, Case, Oliver, and other tractors were arriving from America. Marshalls of Gainsborough were also increasing their production of two stroke "Pop Popping" diesel tractors which were ideal for threshing. The "wind of change was blowing" and the day of the stream threshing engine was "drawing peacefully to its close".

There was, however, one remaining obstacle standing in the way of the change over to tractor power. The steam engines had been developed over many decades to haul the machinery on and off the hard roads and also to drive the threshers on the belt. The imported tractors were good on the road and on the belt but were unable to haul the heavy plant in soft off-the-road conditions as they were not equipped with winches. The Marshall diesels were available with winches but they were not manufactured in sufficient quantities to replace the nation's traction engines immediately. A few manufacturers including "Boughtons" saw and grasped the opportunity to design and build tractor winches. Our years of experience in the timber and threshing industries stood us in good stead, and my brother, who had made winches on a small scale at our Amersham plant since the early 1930s, quickly developed a range which were highly successful. From then on, the fate of the steam threshing engine was sealed.

We took advantage of the glut of new equipment and our good standing with the War Agricultural Committees, to modernise our threshing fleet on advantageous terms.

A line up of some of the Diesels in the Boughton Transport fleet 1945. The author's brother Trafford on extreme left next to our valued friend and revered customer Herbert Grove.

The investment was short lived as Combined Harvesters annihilated the threshing contractors in double quick time as soon as the war was over. In spite of our affection for the steam engines, economic considerations prevailed, and we acquired tractors as fast as practicable. At the end of the war we were operating thirty four sets, (thirty threshing and four clover hulling) twenty five of which were driven by steam, and nine by tractors. Two years later, our threshing drivers had damped down their fires for the last time, as all our sets were tractor driven. Of course, by then the demand for threshing was falling off and fewer sets were needed. By 1950 it was all over for all practical purposes as far as threshing contractors were concerned. The era which had lasted for one hundred years had ended.

The requirement for timber remained brisk for a time and my brother was running thirty-four timber waggons of which thirty-two were diesel and two were steam. Twenty seven operated out of Amersham where we owned electrical sawmills and seven were based near Exeter. He also used sixteen Caterpillar tractors to extract timber from the forests.

The massive slaughter of home grown timber during the war years had taken its toll and as soon as imports could be re-established the demand for round timber haulage fell away and eventually our specialised road haulage business was abandoned and the equipment sold.

Chapter XXII

ADJUSTING TO PEACE TIME

Fowler B.B.1 engines passing through Walkern, Herts with subsoiled plough 1946 Owner T.T.B.

Gearing up to wartime needs is one thing adjusting to peace time conditions is quite another. The war had brought massive changes to the economy and to working practices in the countryside. It was clear that our threshing sets would not be needed for much longer and our forestry transport business had served its purpose. There were on the other hand tremendous opportunities in world markets for equipment of many kinds and we possessed a vast reservoir of "know how" and skill in our ranks of experienced personnel.

A decision was taken to devote our Bell Lane Works to manufacture of capital goods in the realm of mechanical engineering. We had about three years to recover as much of our capital as possible from our investment in agricultural contracting and re-invest the proceeds in machine tools for production. World markets were wide open for our tractor winches and transport equipment, and for a time we had a bonanza.

It was essential that a cash flow should be maintained during the period of transition, and as we had a great deal of goodwill among our farmer customers, we introduced a range of new services to replace the threshing business. These services included crop spraying, the distribution of basic slag and other fertilisers including gas liquor and sludge. We operated combined harvesters and carried out some subsoiling with our steam ploughing engines.

Garrett tractor pulling low loader. Driver "Johnnie" a German P.O.W. from Hanover. Owner T.T.B.

As soon as the war ended, those employees who had joined for the duration returned to their shops, businesses and to the jobs that they were doing before the conflict. They were replaced by men returning from the forces and by German prisoners of war, some of whom settled down in England and made their career with our company.

Our sawmilling interests were developed and my brother and I were supported by Herbert Grove and Philip Hanscomb with whom we created Latimer Sawmills Ltd. which was very successful.

A new company was formed to take care of the Agricultural activities of our business and this was known as Agricultural Enterprises Ltd.. Part of Bovingdon wartime airfield was purchased on which two hangers were situated and this was used as our base for ten years or so until alas, the planning authorities forced us to close it down. The pen had proved mightier than the sword. At a stroke they destroyed our agricultural business which was more than the cut and thrust of competition over sixty years had been able to do.

Meanwhile our manufacturing business at Bell Lane prospered and over a period we built and opened three satellite factories in Devonshire where the authorities made us very welcome.

Chapter XXIII

POST WAR STEAM

Fowler B.B.1. One of six engines purchased for export to British Honduras.

Soon after the war hundreds of fine traction engines were scrapped and no less than thirty five of our engines met this fate. It seemed, at the time, that they were of no further interest to anybody accept the odd eccentric. We kept "Black Jack" and a few other engines for sentimental reasons and other owners did the same.

There were spurts of interest from time to time and I was involved with the export of two pairs of Fowler BBls and implements to British Honduras for a wealthy English business man who wanted them to clear land which he had acquired out there as an investment. He commissioned us to buy six engines.

We bought four engines on his behalf from John Turney who had given up steam dredging by then. One pair were numbered 15418 and 15419 which John had bought from Bletchley Park some years earlier. The other pair were even newer but I have forgotten the numbers. They were fine engines and I did not like to see them go. In addition we bought a fine pair from Ron Ruff of Wilden, Beds but for reasons that I cannot recall, they were never shipped and we bought them back after storing them for some years. After rallying them for many years we sold them to Hardwicks of Ewell, who in turn exported them to Holland where they are in a fine state of preservation.

The harbour at Belize is shallow and on arrival the engines had to be loaded on to lighters. Regrettably the newest pair ended up at the bottom of the sea due to an accident when transferring them to the shore. It was a sad end for such superb engines. I never heard how the customer fared or whether he succeeded in clearing any land.

This photo was taken of an oil painting by the author illustrating his impression of the Fowler BB1 which was sent to France to pull pipelines up the shore for the operation Pluto during World War Two.

At about the same time I was approached by the Colonial Development Corporation to purchase two pairs of BB1 engines with cultivators and a plough for export to the Ground Nut Scheme in Africa. Two pairs from Sussex which had been used during the war to haul Pluto (the pipe line under the Ocean) for the Normandy landings had already been sent out.

Without ado, I travelled to Wiltshire where I knew some engines were standing and bought one pair from Mr. Stratton of Alton Priors and one pair from Mr. Fall of Burbidge Wharf.

All four engines were overhauled by our Amersham works. They looked fine and like new when they were painted and lined. The Burbidge engines were sent out but the other pair were not shipped because the scheme was abandoned and they were not needed. Eventually, one was exported to Montreal, Canada to a steam enthusiast. The other is preserved in the North of England.

Upon arrival in Africa the engines had to be shipped by light railway to the scene of the operations and it was thought that they were too wide to travel on the narrow gauge system. Accordingly they were stripped down in our works and re-assembled on arrival.

Two cultivators were overhauled and were shipped with the engines but they proved to be of limited use as the tines could not cut through the undergrowth.

The plough which we sent to Africa was of particular interest as we converted it from "turn furrows" to discs to deal with the lateral roots which are a feature of the scrub land where the plough was required to operate.

Ransomes of Ipswich supplied the discs and co-operated with us in the development of the implement which was based on a Fowler six furrow anti-balance plough. Trials were conducted at Asheridge Park, Herts using the engines from Alton Priors and after a few modifications the plough performed quite well.

Fowler BB1 which was sent to Africa to work on the Ground Nut Scheme together with the disc plough.

Sentinel "S" Six Wheeler on test. Driven by John Boughton the author. Owner T.T.B.

Foden Six Tonner Overtype demonstrated to the Argentinian Government Representative by the author. Owner T.T.B.

Another time I was asked to demonstrate a steam waggon to a representative from the Argentinian Government. He had already been shown a Sentinel "S" type but wanted to try a Foden overtype for a comparison as he had already been out in a Sentinel. I was happy to oblige.

Mr Thomas T. Boughton (in cap) at the second Appleford Rally chats with Mr. Frank Wilder of Crowmarsh on his left and to Mr. Trafford Boughton on his right whilst Thomas Junior holds his father's hand.

At that time we had five Fodens which we had bought from Fuller Smith & Turner through Mr. Jack Hardwick and I arranged to take the customer for a ride in one of them. My friend John Mullett came along as well. I drove and we took a trip around the villages near where we lived.

All went well and the Argentinian was sufficiently satisfied that steam waggons were what he needed, that he bought sixty or so new Sentinels from the Shrewsbury works to haul coal in his country. From accounts that I have read the coal was of poor quality and the exercise was not entirely satisfactory as it was difficult to maintain a head of steam in the waggons with such inferior fuel.

In due course interest in traction engines as a hobby became popular and the whole preservation movement owes a debt of gratitude to Mr. Napper of Appleford who acted as a catalyst by challenging a friend to a race, using his Marshall as his steed.

The following year four engines took part including a Marshall entered and driven by our friend Esmond Kimbell of Boughton near Northampton. Unfortunately, a hot bearing deprived him of victory. My father's life long friend Frank Wilder of Crowmarsh, Oxfordshire acted as judge and we all went to the rally to see fair play. We have entered engines at rallies all over the South of England ever since. It has been known for one hundred preserved engines to attend a rally and several which we sold for thirty pounds each are now changing hands for tens of thousands of pounds.

For many of us the preservation of steam engines and the many rallies, held all over the country and overseas have brought immense pleasure. The comradeship enjoyed and the lasting friendships formed over many years have been "out of this world". To my good friends Bernard and Cyril Ruff, John and Peter Dickens, Neil Honour, Roy Latchford, David Davis, Jim Hutchins and the countless other volunteers, too numerous to mention, who have unstintingly contributed to the great Steam experience, I say a big thank you, and may God Bless you all.

But wonderful and interesting as the rallies are, they cannot recapture the atmosphere and challenges of steam operations in their hey day. By the time rallies started, the tide had turned. The priorities and pressures of the war years had gone for ever. For those of us who went through the trauma of those hectic years the experience and lessons learned were to prove of immense value in the years ahead.

If our business lives can be compared to a banquet, the narrative so far can be regarded as an aperitif, with many substantial and delectable courses to follow. My brother and I were both still very young and we were not to know that out business would develop to a point where a highly successful range of products would find markets all over the world and involve us in travels to over seventy countries as well as visits to Buckingham Palace and 10, Downing Street, but that is another story.

A group of "Boughton" executives taken at a business conference in the 1980s.

117

Index